A Cosmology for Psychonauts:
Psychophysics, Meditation, and Samadhi

by Shelli Renée Joye

B.S. Electrical Engineering
M.A. Indian Philosophy
Ph.D. Philosophy, Cosmology, and Consciousness

Published by the Viola Institute
Viola, California

2020

Dedicated to my friends and mentors,
Haridas Chaudhuri, John Lilly and
Chögyam Trungpa Rinpoche,
with whom I shared many mind-altering hours of
interchange during the early '70s,
and to Alan Watts who convinced me to move to
California to study Asian philosophy
at the California Institute of Asian Studies in 1974;
and to my amazing wife Susanne Cathryn Rohner,
who encouraged me to begin my PhD program
and subsequently to have the courage to write books.

All rights reserved. No part of this publication may be reproduced, stored in a retrieval system, distributed or transmitted in any form or by any means, without prior written permission in writing of The Viola Institute, or as expressly permitted by law, or under terms agreed with the appropriate reprographic rights organization. Enquiries concerning reproduction outside the scope of the above should be sent to The Viola Institute at the above address.

Some of the material in this book has appeared previously in my books *The Acquisition of Supersensible Perception.*

Copyright © 2020 The Viola Institute

Printed in the United States of America

**A Cosmology for Psychonauts:
Psychophysics, Meditation, and Samadhi**

ISBN: 978-1-950761-05-0

OTHER BOOKS BY THE SAME AUTHOR:

Developing Supersensible Perception: Knowledge of the Higher Worlds through Entheogens, Prayer, and Nondual Awareness

Tuning the Mind: Geometries of Consciousness

Exploring the Noosphere: Teilhard de Chardin

The Little Book of Consciousness: Holonomic Brain Theory and the Implicate Order

The Electromagnetic Brain: EM Field Theories on the Nature of Consciousness

Sub-Quantum Consciousness: A Geometry of Consciousness Based Upon the Work of Karl Pribram, David Bohm, and Pierre Teilhard de Chardin

Introduction

The primary intent of this book is to describe in some detail the author's own personal experience and interpretation of contemplative practice over a fifty year period of psychonautical exploration both with entheogens as well as through practical experience in the practices taught by numerous Asian and Western mystical traditions. As a young electrical engineering student, I had the good fortune to experience the effects induced through ingesting a large dose of LSD-25 at night on a beach in California. The effect of the experiences that night immediately changed the course of my life as I became fascinated with consciousness and how I might be able to eventually understand how one's individual awareness could move through so many seemingly disparate dimensions of reality, many of them far different than offered my "normal" human daily awareness.

Over the next several years, while trying to learn more about consciousness and how it might manifest in the cosmos from a scientific viewpoint, I discovered the many ways that had been developed over the centuries by mystics, saints, and shamans worldwide for exploring consciousness. In order to explore the subject as deeply as possible, I entered a Master of Arts program in Asian Studies where I focused upon Indian philosophy and studied the Sanskrit language in order to translate Patanjali's *Yoga Sutras* and other important texts that had been developed over the centuries by psychonauts in the Indian subcontinent.

I categorized all of these techniques under the term "psychonautics" to indicate the exploration of new worlds of consciousnes experientially, much as early nautical exploration had been conducted on our planet over the past five centuries.

The major section of this book describes both what I have learned and how I approached psychonautics.

The final part of the book, the Appendix, is a more technical description of the cosmology of consciousness, taken from a paper that I presented at a professional conference on consciousness several years ago in Berkeley, California.

A Cosmology for Psychonauts

Psychophysics, Meditation, and Samadhi

By Shelli Renee Joye, BSEE, MA, PhD

How the world (our One universe, our Self) is structured; the geometry of our cosmos and how to navigate within it.

In contemporary culture the word *meditation*, following its traditional meaning, is invariably associated with practices that are embedded within a particular religion. Popular opinion holds that the practice of meditation can lead to a state of peace and tranquility or even to some rare mystical "enlightenment experiences" in which one feels to have expanded one's consciousness to include a sense of being "one with" or in "communion with" with a higher "Being" or simply the widely used none, "God."[1] This discussion offers practical techniques of meditation, extracted from Indian, Tibetan, and Christian traditions, presented here for those interested in developing or enhancing their own specific approaches to their private practice. I will focus primarily upon my own story, my own somewhat unique daily practices, sharing my general approach to meditation and describing in some detail my own first-hand experiences. But to begin with, it may be useful for readers to understand the difference between the use of the word "meditation" and the word "contemplation."

In the Middle Ages, the prolific[2] religious writer Hugh of Saint Victor (1096-1141), in trying to put more structure into the monastic approaches to meditation, wrote that there are three possible activities or states of the soul (individual human consciousness):

- thinking,
- meditation, and
- contemplation.

European monastics tended to emphasize *meditation*, the second of these three states of brain-mind, an approach which included a focus upon communal and individual recitation of prayer sequences as well as reading the scriptures and spiritual texts very slowly with great focus of attention upon the meanings of words.[3] Hugh's third state of awareness, contemplation or *contemplatio*, described a practice of cognitive silence and divine listening that, as a portal to psychonautic exploration, was understood to be a more direct approach to the experience of God, as contrasted with meditation, the effort exercised within intermediate stages between normal everyday consciousness and the psychonautic oceans that one finds oneself entering within the higher stages of contemplation. Techniques[4] of meditation were understood as intermediary and leading up to the third state in which consciousness entered contemplation, that developed into the high art of what we would call psychonautics.

There are a wide range of techniques of prayer and meditation that have been developed within numerous cultural tradition. Perhaps the most important validation is that of direct experience. This book does not deal directly with psychophysics but describes the author's own specific experiences and practices that have evolved during my fifty years of introspective[5] exploration of the many Tantric[6] techniques described in earlier books by the same author.

First it should be noted that without thinking about it too much, over the years I have adopted "what works" into my daily contemplative meditation sessions. By no means am I suggesting that anyone interested in contemplative practice should copy my own sequence of practices. However if it is true that every person's life and persona is the unique product of a particular era, family, society, and educational background, then it should be apparent that every person can and should discover "what works for them" by actually trying a range of different practices, even perhaps re-visiting techniques they learned as children from within their own particular family, religion, and culture (i.e., prayers, rituals, etc.).

The rest of my discussion here will be rather informal as it will reflect my attempt to convey material that others might find of use in the development of ones own unique approach to an effective Tantric psychonautic contemplative practice. Much of the material will be of an auto-biographical nature.

Early Contemplative Experiences

I first became serious in exploring contemplation shortly after graduating from an engineering program, had moved to New York City and become interested in *Hatha Yoga* practice. One late evening I was in the quiet windowless inner room of my 5th floor walk-up in the Lower East Side of Manhattan doing my usual stretching exercises, trying to maintain a shoulder stand posture (*sarvāṅgāsana*) for 10 minutes as part of my *hatha yoga* practice. Part of the exercise was to move into the pose, then to become as quiet as possible, practicing internal silence. This required making an effort to attenuate every thoughts that might arise, to detach from and not follow memories as they began to form, nor to allow any inner dialogue to resume streaming. The goal was to open up the bandwidth of awareness and to remain receptive, just listening. Suddenly, out of the silence, I heard a singular loud, high pitched tone which seemed to be located somewhere within my cranium. I noticed that as I focused my awareness on the sound it seemed to coalesce into a point while substantially increasing in volume! I quickly feared I might be experiencing a brain aneurism in progress. But as I soon discovered that by maintaining my focus, I was able to coax the sound into growing louder and more distinct, my fears were transformed into awe at this audible tone coming from within. Even more strange was that accompanying the sound sensation was a sensation of "touch" detectible within this tiny region located somewhere within the upper right-hand quadrant of my brain.

Then things became even more strange. After noticing the initial "bright" sound, additional "points" of sound of distinctly different pitch began to rise into awareness *in other locations in my cranium.* I gently lowered myself from my shoulder-stand position and, ending my hatha yoga for the night, lay down under a blanket in the dark. For many hours that night I could not sleep, totally fascinated in focusing upon and listening to the sounds that would variously increase in volume according to the degree that I would be able to direct my attention toward them. I noticed, however, that as soon as I would begin consciously thinking "about them" or "thinking in words," letting my attention begin to stray, they would subside and contact would be lost. I quickly learned that by gently dropping my train of thought which seemed so insistent on thinking, classifying, etc., I was able once more enter the silence and the tiny sounds would suddenly peek out of the silence once more, and increase in volume in what was clearly a feedback loop, a sort of reverberation responding to my search. The tones were quite pure, high pitched, and I suppose most people would classify them as a "ringing in the ears." Several months later I discovered the term "tinnitus," which was defined by medical science as any perceived sound not brought in by the ear canal. Since perception of these sounds seemed to bother people, doctors decided that it must be an disease of the hearing system with an unknown (yet to be determined) source.

Nevertheless, by now being quite serious in my efforts to explore the phenomenon of "consciousness" by any means possible, I was completely fascinated by what was happening that night in my top floor apartment. I found that by trying to ignore a particularly dominant bright sound and trying to focus on a fainter, more obscure sound ("further away from" or "behind" the first) the second sound would immediately grow louder in volume and become easier to focus upon using this inner focal-sense mechanism. Here was direct cause and effect, albeit in an internal domain of consciousness among some kind of living experiential fields of energy dynamics. All that night I lay awake in the dark, moving from sound to sound within my head, as each would rise and fall, almost as if each had an independent volition of its own. I experienced strong emotional oscillations between exaltation verging on disbelief, and terror that I might be damaging my neuronal centers, perhaps even encouraging (or experiencing) a brain damaging hemorrhage.

As an electrical engineer, I had often listened to various single sinusoidal tones generated by equipment in laboratory sessions, yet this was not a single tone but a confluence of tones faintly making up a background of the perceived, sensed audio range, like those aforementioned "peepers" in the forest at night at Hamilton's pool. It was at specific points in space within my cranium, that from time to time a tone would arise with exponential sharpness high above the background level, to become a bright point, like a beacon, upon which, if I were able to sustain focus for a few moments, would become markedly louder with an accompanying intense tactile sensation.

During the course of what seemed a very long night my body grew hot and sweated profusely, soaking the sheets in what I assumed might be a fever caused by whatever was happening in my brain. I went through what seemed to be a long period of deep fear, suspecting that I had somehow damaged my nervous system. Yet, since that first night listening to the inner sounds, I have never experienced a headache or discomfort of any kind within my cranium.

Some time in the early morning hours I fell asleep. When I awoke it was with great relief to find that my mind seemed to be back to normal, having returned to its familiar mode of verbalized thoughts, chatting away merrily once more. However I now lived with these new memories and realization that something singularly strange had occurred, something I had never been prepared for and which I had never previously encountered in books nor in life's experiences.

I continued to practice *hatha yoga* but spent increasingly long periods in silent meditation, finding that, now, I was able to fairly easily contact these resonant inner sounds. I began the practice of focusing upon them while falling asleep, and found that when I would begin to awaken from a dream in the middle of the night, I was able to quickly re-enter the dream world by following these mysterious bright inner sounds.

My training in physics and electrical engineering led me to believe that these internal sounds were sine waves, not some sort of random noise. The tones also appeared to manifest in narrow spectrums centered about fundamental frequencies. For a time, I conjectured that they might be mechanical resonances within the physical structures of my inner ear. At the time I worked as an engineer in a large building in lower Manhattan and began to experience, with great surprise, one of the high pitched sounds flare up in my cranium whenever I approached certain electronic equipment, computer screens, or even certain vending machines. At such moments I found myself internally verbalizing, with some humor "incoming," a phrase widely heard in the media at that time, from the front lines in Vietnam.

Over the next few weeks I noticed that, during my meditation sessions, if I concentrated awareness within different physical/spatial locations within my body, such as the heart or the throat, perceptually different sounds would arise in different locations and patterns, though the sounds were most clear and pronounced in the central region of my brain.

I soon concluded that the source of these perceived inner sounds must be of an electromagnetic nature, possibly the vibrations of a neuronal plexus within my nervous system resonating with electromagnetic modulations of our Earth's electromagnetic energy fields, or in the case of vending machines, the harmonic frequencies of some internal electrical radiation emanating from their circuitry, transformers, etc.

In bookstores I began to browse through books on anatomical structures of the brain and the central nervous system. This was the age before the internet, but luckily I was living in New York City, and had access not only to the New York Public Library, but to many bookstores with medical sections. I was soon able to obtain excellent material with technical illustrations and x-ray photographs of internal physiological structures. I used these to visualize, with as much detail as possible, those internal areas, usually corresponding with the Indian chakra system, while meditating in the dark.

Over several years this process, concentrating and visualizing within areas of my body and focusing on the sound tones as they would arise, became a main source of meditative practice for me, and the inner sounds tones grew ever more richly complex and often markedly louder in volume, and began to produce distinct tactile sensations of flowing nature, unlike the sensations felt in the external senses of touch, vision, taste, and hearing.

On weekends I would also search for books for guidance in silent meditation, and in the process discovered the *Patañjali's Yoga Sūtras*. My first copy was a translation with commentaries by Professor Ernest E. Wood (1883–1965), having the rather impressive (and long) title of *Practical Yoga, Ancient and Modern, Being a New, Independent Translation of Patañjali's Yoga Aphorisms, Interpreted in the Light of Ancient and Modern Psychological Knowledge and Practical Experience.*

I was thoroughly impressed that Wood had first been educated in the "hard" sciences of chemistry, physics and geology, and only later had he become so thoroughly fascinated by yoga and meditation that he undertook to become a Sanskrit scholar. Wood's translations of the Sūtras seemed to me to be the perfect manual for the type of meditative exploration that had become my passion. After carefully studying Wood's translation for several months, I found a different translation of the *Yoga Sūtras* by a professor holding a PhD in chemistry, Dr. I.K. Taimni (1898–1978).[3] To my surprise, many of the translations and commentaries differed markedly between the two books. This led me to attempt an understanding of each word in the context of my own experiences and practices.

Common Elements for Beginning Psychonauts

Several basic considerations for achieving the ability to enter the "inner silence" that is the beginning state of psychonautic exploration are as follows:

- Having a special place, a *temenos*[7] where you can "sit" and practice contemplation in relative silence free of distraction.
- A regular, preferably daily sessions with a minimum time goal (beginners often try for 10 minutes, experienced contemplatives can "sit" for 30 minutes, extremely

advanced adepts can "sit" for multiple hours without interruption).
- Practicing at the same time period of the day (early morning, sunset, or midnight).

Meditation Sitting on a Cushion (Zafu)

While one can certainly practice some forms of meditation while walking or lying down (though falling asleep can become a problem), most schools of meditation begin by suggesting the practitioner sit cross-legged close to the floor upon a stuffed cushion, called a *zafu* in Japanese. I have several zafu cushions of various color and fillings, but the key is to "sit" on a cushion daily, preferably at the same time period so that the body-mind-consciousness becomes used to the position and recognizes it and the associated activity which is expected (contemplative exercises, psychonautical exploration, indescribable journeys).

It is also suggested to put the zafu in the center of a wide flat cushion called a *zabuton* so your feet, ankles and legs rest on a nice padded area, not on a cold hard floor. To meditate when travelling and in a hotel room, I sit upon two pillows from the bed upon a folded blanket

The key is to sit on the cushion or pillows and teach yourself how to meditate simply *by trying to meditate*. As in many things in life, you learn most by direct experience. For example in learning to ride a bicycle, nobody can really teach you, but can only encourage you (especially when you fall down) as you *teach yourself* how to ride by re-programming your mind-body of brain, muscles, and nerves. Although meditation is primarily a matter of learning through experience, here are a few additional tips that have worked well for me. Most spiritual progress results from *trying* various written or oral teachings, and in particular *not* just trying once or twice, but to give any particular technique a real chance to "grow." To begin to appreciate any new practice, as in learning to ride a bicycle, requires some actual repetition over at least several weeks. This gives the cognitive mind-brain the chance to learn, program, and thus create new relatively permanent skills within itself through neuroplasticity.[8]

Find an area of about 36" along your floorboard that is clear of furniture. Or just use a clear area in the middle of the room. If you place the zabuton against the wall, leave about six inches of floor where you can place a candle of small lamp if you like. Place the zafu on the zabuton (or place the thicker pillows upon a folded blanket).

Use a timer. When I first began to practice meditation, I set a small timer for 10 minutes. Now in 2020, I often use a free iPhone app called "Insight Timer"[9] though there are many others currently available. The best times to meditate, according to many traditions, are during the four geophysical transitions: dawn, noon, sunset, and midnight.

But I find I can enter the various contemplative stages at any time of the day as long as the room is quite dark and there is not much ambient noise. Years ago I discovered that earplugs are useful to block out any random external noise, and they work quite well, once you get used to inserting them comfortably. They are also great if your companion snores!

Meditative Time Duration

For many months I found it quite difficult to suspend my thoughts in silence for the full ten minutes. Also I would not practice every day, sometimes weeks would go by, but then I began discovering, or suspecting, various "benefits" of entering the silence.

By just focusing within an area (*chakra* region) and sustaining that state of focus for at least 30 seconds, I would suddenly begin to sense a new, often unexpectedly perceivable sensation within those areas of my body.

Within a few months of beginning to practice, I set a goal to be able to practice for 30 minutes. To my surprise it took a few years before I was able to practice comfortably for up to 30 minutes, but then everyone will progress at a different rate. When we lived in the silent desert community of Abqaiq, Saudi Arabia, I managed to reach 60 minute sessions now and then, but today I find 30 minutes is fine to "keep me charged," to allow me to connect with the deeper Self, and to practice psychonautic exploration. It is not the time *elapsed* that is most important but the *quality of one's attention*, one's sustained focus, during whatever time period has been set.

Warming Up the Chakras

The skill of supersensible perception initially grows fairly quickly if you are able to direct your attention on various internal regions of your physiology. It helps to be able to visualize these internal regions three-dimensionally, and to this end it is good to spend time looking through the internet or at drawings, sketches, and photographic images commonly found in a wide range of medical textbooks. Through earnest attempts to visualize and to tactilely feel these internal physiological regions (e.g., the ventricular cavities visualized in the brain within the skull, the heart and its region, etc.) one will eventually begin to feel something new in these regions, a sense of immediate warming, some kind of activation or subtle vibration. In my own practice I have focused on eight of these regions that are known classically as "the *chakras*," and in any one 30 minutes session (or at the beginning, 10 minute sessions) I would usually pick only one center to focus upon/within. However there if I am practicing with a *mantra*, I usually use each syllable of the *mantra* to focus on a specific *chakra* briefly, before moving to the next syllable of the *mantra* and shift my focus to the next physiologically-centered *chakra*.

The physiological basis of "warming up the *chakras*" can be understood in the same way as biofeedback can be used to make one's fingertips (or the tip of one's nose) warmer. When my son was 12 he entered a science fair project exploring biofeedback. The objective of the project was to show how one could raise the temperature of a single fingertip by focusing awareness on the area for several minutes. We were both surprised at the results of his project during which we learned that at during the first week of daily attempts to raise the fingertip temperature, no change was recorded. However on about the tenth day my fingertip temperature rose by one and a half degrees Fahrenheit, and on the 12th day my son's also increase by one degree. After a month of trying every day for about ten minutes, we were both able to increase our fingertip temperature by over two degrees, and sometimes three degrees. The explanation was that through practice (and neuroplasticity) the focus of efferent neurons within an area, say the center of the head, or the throat, or the heart, causes capillaries to expand in diameter which increases the capillary blood flow, increases the "heat" (infrared) and increases the rate of oxygenation and cleaning of the region of focus. This in turn seems to stimulate the afferent neuronal tracts with the effect that you begin to *feel* the region more distinctly as your awareness seems to flow into it and back in a sort of sensory feedback loop. I think, if nothing else, it is a really good way of taking care of internal systems, letting them warm up and relax and operate at a beneficial level.

Repetition of Prayer/Mantra

At times you might want to practice silent prayer or *mantra*. One way of looking at prayers and *mantras* is to see them as verbal tools that are used to keep verbal consciousness from wandering into regions of the mind that trigger new streams of thought, and thus distract from going into deeper levels of contemplative psychonautics. For example, the traditional Russian Orthodox practice (known as *hesychia*) is quite often taught as a focus of awareness within an area of the abdomen, a region that is similar to the Japanese *hara* region upon which martial artists focus. *Hesychasts* maintain this focus while repeating a Christian *mantra* known as the "Jesus Prayer." A contemporary practice among some Roman Catholic groups is to repeat the Aramaic word *"maranatha"* while maintaining focus with the heart region of the chest.[10]

Meditation Sequence

The sequence of my own meditation? I usually prepare by finding an interesting metaphysical, psychology, or philosophical book and then, sitting on the zafu (or two pillows in a hotel room), I read for a few minutes from a spiritual text (e.g., the *Holy Bible*, the *Holy Koran,* the *Psalms,* the *Bhagavad Gita,* the *Philokalia,* etc.) or from a book on contemplation or an essay by a monk and occasionally a poem. This acts as a transition from active, everyday cognitive thinking and allows my emotional being to move toward a more spiritual, psychonautic, silent state of awareness. After ten minutes or so of reading, I often smoke a small amount of cannabis (and light a bit of incense). I almost always also have a cup of tea or strong hot coffee within reach, which I occasionally sip, even during the contemplative session. Then I blow out the candle if one were lit. While thinking of people I love and have loved and care and have cared about, those who have died and those still alive, I say a few prayers for several minutes, often repeating ten times while focusing/counting on each finger in sequence. In many cultures this is done with some form of prayer beads such as the rosary in Catholicism, the "worry beads" in Islam, or 108 bead *malas* used by Hindus and Buddhists. Some of the prayers are of Roman Catholic origin (Our Father and Hail Mary in English, sometimes in Latin), others are Russian Orthodox or the few Sanskrit mantras I have memorized and work with, or even a single word *Maranatha* such as is taught by several Catholic monks, which is Aramaic for "Come Lord."

The prayer period is just a period of transition from normal mental cognition and ideation to the "sitting consciousness" mode. It also brings a sense (and reality) of communion with all our ancestors (and contemporaries) who have said the same sequence of words, whether prayer or *mantra*, with similar intentions. Frequency vibrations go out into the universe of space-time as well as into the frequency domain, where they resonate with similar or identical vibrations. Like tuning in to a reliably good "station," one's prayer/*mantra* joins with the vibrant energy of every individual who has ever uttered the same frequency pattern, either audibly or mentally. Teilhard de Chardin might say that such prayer repetition leads us to resonate with and to join the noosphere[11] during contemplative sessions, tuning in to the collective harmonics of all who have gone before and all who are currently consciously alive.

As the prayer minutes fall away, I select an area of focus, shifting my attention away from the verbal, in an intentional, physical way. Often my focus is the heart region (suggested by the Buddhist *Heart Sutra*, or the Christian "Sacred Heart of Jesus.") I just try to feel the area of the heart as I simultaneously make an effort to refrain from "remembering" anything (other than concentrating on the heart), to immediately banish (if possible) unbidden thoughts, memories of things I might need to do, and short term memories of recent activities earlier in the day, doing my best to detach from any such distraction as they arise.

Quieting the cognitive mind is surprisingly difficult in the beginning, but eventually one develops the skill and capability to quickly "let go" of unbidden thoughts, no matter how tempting. You can think of it as saving brain "battery power." As less energy is used by the brain-mind to manipulate complex thoughts and retrieve and process memories, this energy accumulates. This can be of great advantage for creativity but also a danger to continued progress in meditation. As one gains skill in quieting the mind and mental "energy reserves" builds up, so too does the pressure for a newly created thought to emerge. If one follows that thought, then the forward progress in meditation is broken as mental activities currently in a state of suspension now spring into activity to analyze, support, enhance the new thought, while activating the memory system in order to store the thought. You might visualize the problem in the image of a subway car that you are riding in with your goal being to not stop until you reach a far away station, but suddenly your subway car pulls into an intermediary station that has features that capture your attention and you are tempted to get off the train at this station, giving up the opportunity to persevere and remain on the train until you reach the more distant, original goal.

At some point in your session as you listen, new dimensions will slowly unfold to your internal awareness as your sensitivity and skill of tuning into them increases with time and practice. You will begin to experience unusual sensations, sometimes hearing unusually pure sound frequencies, or the distinct sensation of *flow* of some liquid or plasma in various regions of your head, chest, or abdomen. You may begin to experience flashes of what feel (or sound) like electrical discharges, a high pitched electrical crackling sound or sensation in your cranium, just beneath the bone of the skull. And this is just the beginning!

Afterword

I hope that my efforts here will encourage readers to practice meditation and contemplation either as beginners or with renewed enthusiasm, as I know it will enrich your life in many ways, and I believe your efforts, and all of our efforts, collectively, will work to heal yourself, our community of human beings on Earth, and the planet itself.

APPENDIX
The Cosmology of Consciousness

By Shelli Renee Joye

In this Appendix, the cosmology of consciousness is described in the holoflux theory of consciousness, a modulated consciousness-energy shown to support both local and non-local properties. This hypothesis emerges from an integral evaluation of evidence drawn from: (1) the holonomic mind/brain theories of Karl Pribram, (2) the ontological interpretation of quantum theory by David Bohm. Applying an integral methodology to superimpose and correlate seemingly disparate concepts from among these sources and others, a composite theory emerges, a "holoflux" theory of consciousness, after the term favored by Karl Pribram to describe David Bohm's "holomovement" between an explicate order and an implicate order. This Pribram–Bohm composite holoflux theory is shown to be congruent with established principles of physics, mathematics, and electrical engineering.

Extending the panpsychist paradigm that consciousness is inherent in the structure of the universe, the theory describes a dynamic energy process bridging the explicate space–time domain with a transcendent flux domain located at the spatial center, everywhere. This center is hypothesized to be synonymous with Karl Pribram's "flux domain" and David Bohm's "implicate order."

Extending the theories of Pribram and Bohm, the holoflux hypothesis maps reality as a nondual energy, cycling mathematically, lens-like, in a process of transformation manifesting in three modes: (1) electromagnetic energy in space–time, (2) holoflux energy in a transcendent order, and (3) vibrating isospheres at the boundary gap separating the implicate from the explicate orders.

Perhaps the most widely debated issue in consciousness studies can be found encapsulated in the phrase "the hard problem of consciousness," first articulated in an essay by David Chalmers (1995) in which he discusses consciousness as experience. A product of our digital age, Chalmers understandably conflates experience with information processing, but questionably suggests that it is information processing itself that gives rise to experience:

> The really hard problem of consciousness is the problem of experience. When we think and perceive, there is a whir of information processing, but there is also a subjective aspect.... Why should physical processing give rise to a rich inner life at all? It seems objectively unreasonable that it should, and yet it does. If any problem qualifies as the problem of consciousness, it is this one. (p. 5)

Chalmers (1995) here places the cart before the horse if he really means to say that consciousness arises from information processing. That would make consciousness an epiphenomenon, something that arises from what he calls the "whir of information processing." What he seems to be addressing is the hard problem of mind, rather than the hard problem of consciousness. More recently, however, Chalmers (2010) has suggested that consciousness may not be derivative after all, that it may be seen as "fundamental" in the same sense as space and time are regarded by physicists as "fundamental."

Like epiphenomenalism, other assumptions restrict the range of contemporary approaches to consciousness research, and may accordingly be similarly misleading, for example (a) the assumption that the word consciousness is limited specifically to "human consciousness," and (b) the assumption that consciousness is a phenomenon exclusive to the space-time continuum.

Understandably, such assumptions have arisen due to a widespread fascination with hardware, and in particular the hardware of the brain, fostered by an approach to science which limits itself to measurements which can be observed in space–time. Thus epiphenomenalism has become mainstream, reinforced by such statements as the following, found in Gerald Edelman and Giulio Tononi's (2000) conclusion to their book, *A Universe of Consciousness*, where they observe:

> Consciousness while special, arose as a result of evolutionary innovations in the morphology of the brain and body. The mind arises from the body and its development; it is embodied and therefore part of nature. . . . We have argued throughout this book that

consciousness arises from certain arrangements in the material order of the brain. (pp. 215–219)

If the word consciousness in Edelman and Tononi's (2000) quote could be replaced with "the mind," or "human mental cognition," the observation might be less problematic, but to state that consciousness arises from the brain is questionable. This essay takes the opposite view, that the human mind, mental cognition, the operational processes of the brain arises from consciousness, that they are not the same thing.

Nor is consciousness necessarily limited to space, or restricted in time, nor exclusive to human primates. Descriptions of mystical and religious experiences handed down by every culture provide strong evidence that there exist modes of consciousness that can be explored beyond normal waking thought; all traditions offer prayer, contemplation, and the ingestion of psychotropic plant substances as doorways to experience beyond space and time (Bellah, 2011). Additional evidence is close at hand—the universal nightly human experience of dream states—which seem not necessarily to be a product of normally experienced time, space, or mental cognition.

It is evident that serious efforts have indeed been made to explore consciousness in order to discover the outlines of an architecture of consciousness through first-hand experience. In support of such efforts, and to counter the epiphenomenalist turn in consciousness studies, this paper offers a model of consciousness that builds upon the ideas of the theoretical physicist David Bohm (1980) and the neuroscientist Karl Pribram (2013).

BACKGROUND: The Pribram-Bohm Holoflux Topology

The topological model which is developed here in support of a metaverse cosmology is presented in Figure 1, the "Pribram-Bohm Holoflux Model," where the basic theory is diagrammed as consciousness transforming between nonlocal and local regions of experience and information (Joye, in press).

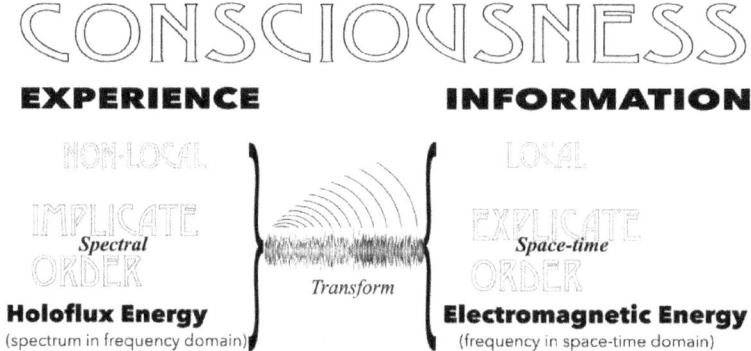

Figure 1. The Pribram-Bohm holoflux model

The Pribram-Bohm hypothesis regards consciousness as a cybernetic energy process, a holoflux transforming between two orders of being in "an undivided flowing movement without borders" (Bohm, 1980, p. 172). To the left in the diagram of Figure 1, consciousness is expressed as a spectrum of holoflux energy in Bohm's implicate order. This holoflux energy resonates with electromagnetic energy of the same frequencies to the right in the diagram, in the space-time region, or explicate order (Bohm, 1980, p. 159).

Viewed from left to right, the diagram reveals a spectrum of holoflux energy in the transcendental implicate order transforming and translated into "things" and "events" in local space-time, and conversely, viewing the diagram from right to left, information generated by "things" and "events" interacting throughout space-time is seen to be transforming (folding) back into the implicate order. The process is described as a continuous cybernetic cycle, perhaps occurring at a regular clock-rate.

Superposition of Consciousness: Cybernetics and the Fourier Transform

Common experience would suggest that all consciousness is consciousness *of* something, such as the experience of a sound, of an image, of a sensation, of an emotion, of an interior verbal thought. These experiences seem to be superpositioned, they often occur at what seem to be the same perceptual moment. Yet each simultaneous stream of experience remains distinct, somehow integrated with all the others. But what is it that is "looking at" this stream of experiences? It is as if there is some meta-consciousness that is more than the sum of each of these individual "experience streams," per se, but rather some other, more comprehensive level, some panoramic perspective that is able to embrace and comprehend them all, and which has the amazing ability to *fine tune* its own selected focus upon *one or more* of these streams of awareness while simultaneously dampening and filtering out the many others.

In signal analysis this stream phenomenon is explained by the *superposition principle*, formalized in

1822 by the French mathematician Jean-Baptiste Fourier, who developed the mathematics of what is now called "Fourier analysis" during his search for a mathematical relationship between space-time and frequency (Feynman, Leighton, & Sands, 1964, p. 286). Because signals are more readily superpositioned and manipulated (filtered, amplified, etc.) within the *frequency domain* than in the *time domain*, the Fourier transform equations have become primary and ubiquitous mathematical tools in physics and engineering for analyzing, synthesizing, and transmitting signals between two domains:

a "space-time domain (t_d)," and

a "frequency domain (f_d)."

Much of electrical engineering circuit design is done within the frequency domain, and only subsequently implemented with time domain components, as described here by Francis F. Kuo, chief electrical engineer at the original Bell Telephone Laboratory from which emerged the transistor, the laser, and radio astronomy, information theory, and the Unix operating system. In his textbook on *Network Analysis and Synthesis*, Kuo (1962) states:

We see that in the **time domain** (i.e., where the independent variable is **t**) the voltage–current relationships are given in terms of differential equations. On the other hand, in the complex **frequency domain**, the voltage–current relationships for the elements are expressed in **algebraic** equations. Algebraic equations are, in most cases, more easily solved than differential equations. Herein lies the **raison d'être** for describing signals and networks in the frequency domain as well as in the time domain. (p. 13)

Norbert Wiener (1948) coined the term "cybernetics" from the Greek κυβερνήτης—"steersman, governor, pilot, or rudder" (p. 11)—during his own work at the same Bell Telephone Laboratory as Kuo, and made use of Fourier's transform to model and analyze brain waves in the frequency domain, where he discovered clear evidence of the existence of "self-organization of electroencephalograms or brain waves" (p. 181). Using Fourier analysis, an approach which later became of great interest to Bohm, Wiener (1948) was able to detect uniquely narrow frequency ranges, centered within different spatial locations on the cortex, that repeatedly exhibited auto-correlation (p. 191). Regions on the cortex were identified where specific ranges of frequencies were found to coalesce toward intermediate frequencies, seeming both to attract and to strengthen one another, exhibiting *resonance* or "self tuning" to amplify and consolidate signals into narrowly specific ranges in the frequency domain f_d (p. 198). His research led Wiener to conjecture that the *infrared band* of electromagnetic flux may be the loci of "self–organizing systems":

> We thus see that a nonlinear interaction causing the attraction of frequency can generate a self–organizing system, as it does in the case of the brain waves we have discussed . . . This possibility of self-organization is by no means limited to the very low frequency of these two phenomena. Consider self–organizing systems at the frequency level, say, of infrared light. (p. 202)

Three years after Wiener's (1948) publication of *Cybernetics*, David Bohm (1951) stressed the importance of Fourier's equations on the first page of his well-received 646-page textbook, *Quantum Theory*, where he encouraged a familiarity with Fourier analysis for an ontological understanding of quantum phenomena:

> It seems impossible to develop quantum concepts extensively without Fourier analysis. It is, therefore, presupposed that the reader is moderately familiar with Fourier analysis. (p. 1)

For purposes of this paper, the basic understanding of Fourier analysis is simply that *frequency vibrations* manifest within two distinct dimensions or domains: a space-time domain and a frequency domain. Until recently, physicists have focused exclusively within space-time to conduct their research, considering only space and time as having any "reality" and considering the ontological reality of the frequency domain, if at all, in the same vague category as the domain of mathematics itself (i.e., in some unspecified transcendent dimension). Whether there might somehow exist a "real" dimension *outside of* space-time, or beyond space-time has generally been beyond the purview of the physical sciences. Yet the experienced reality of a region of consciousness beyond space-time is supported by the vast body of first-hand reports generated by religious, mystical, or near-death experiences. In an approach to such experiences, William James (1902/2004), the "father of American psychology," writes:

> The further limits of our being plunge, it seems to me, into an altogether other dimension of existence from the sensible and merely "understandable" world. Name it the mystical region, or the supernatural region, whichever you choose. So far as our ideal impulses originate in this region (and most of them do originate in it, for we find them possessing us in a way for which we cannot articulately account), we belong to it in a more intimate sense than that in which we belong to the visible world, for we belong in the most intimate sense wherever our ideals belong. (p. 318)

Fourier's transform equations (Figure 2) between the two domains of time (t_d) and frequency (f_d) are more than simply mathematical equations, written down as functions in the abstract symbolic language of calculus (Stein & Shakarchi, 2003, pp. 134–36).

$$f(t) = \int_{-\infty}^{+\infty} X(F)e^{j2\pi Ft} dF \qquad f(F) = \int_{-\infty}^{+\infty} x(t)e^{-j2\pi Ft} dt$$

Fourier integral transform of a continuous frequency function into the time domain (t_d).

Fourier integral transform of a continuous time function into the frequency domain (F_d).

Figure 2. The Fourier transform and inverse transform (Kuo, 1962)

These two expressions indicate that any function in the timespace domain, $f(t)$, can be transformed into and expressed equivalently as an infinite series of frequency spectra functions $X(F)$ in the frequency domain. The transformation is also possible in the opposite direction, such that any arbitrary function in the frequency domain, $f(F)$ can be transformed into and expressed by an infinite series of time functions, $x(t)$. The two domains mirror one another.

Beyond purely mathematical considerations, the equations can be taken as models of an actual cosmic process (i.e., much as Newton's Law model the phenomenon of gravity) and they can be understood as mirroring the cosmos in mathematical terms. The model of consciousness presented in this paper proposes that there is indeed an ontological reality to this other region, and that this region is synonymous with Bohm's "implicate order," Pribram's "holonomic frequency domain."

Karl Pribram's Holonomic Mind/Brain Theory: The Frequency Domain

The neurosurgeon Karl Pribram (1971) was one of the first to articulate the idea that the Fourier transform might play a role in brain/mind neurophysics. Pribram (1990) spent decades performing laboratory research to gather experimental data in an effort to solve two problems: (a) to identify the location and mechanism of memory storage (the *engram*), and (b) to discover the cognitive mechanism behind visual perception. Pribram (2013) arrived at the conclusion that the data revealed evidence of Fourier signal transformations of visual signals from the rods and cones of the eyes, and that these Fourier patterns could be detected in spatial Fourier patterns over wide areas of the brain, as fields within the fine-fibered dendritic networks of the cerebral cortex (p. 82).

In the mid-1960s, Pribram was inspired by reports of the first optical holograms, and the empirical evidence that holograms could store, retrieve, and process vast quantities of information using resonant photons in high frequency beams. Ten years later, Pribram (1971) published *Languages of the Brain*, in which he detailed his new theory, the holonomic brain/mind theory, based upon evidence of the Fourier transform playing a key role in the mind/brain process. The theory he put forth proposed that the cognitive sensory processes of memory, sight, hearing, and consciousness in general, may all operate holographically, in a transformational process of information-coded-energies flowing back and forth between space–time and the frequency domain via a Fourier transform mechanism.

Pribram's (1971) theory was radical and controversial, challenging two prominent paradigms of modern neurophysical research: (a) the belief that consciousness is an epiphenomenon produced by electrical sparks among synaptic–clefts throughout the wiring of neurons the brain, and (b) the belief that somewhere in the physical brain, *engrams* of memory are stored, and will be eventually found. Pribram (1971) relates a story of a conversation he had at the time, while climbing with colleagues on a hike in Colorado just prior to attending a neuroscience conference in Boulder:

> We had climbed high into the Rocky Mountains. Coming to rest on a desolate crag, a long meditative silence was suddenly broken by a query from Campbell: "Karl, do you really believe it's a Fourier?" I hesitated, and then replied, "No Fergus, that would be too easy, don't you agree?" Campbell sat silently awhile, then said, "You are right, it's probably not that easy. So what are you going to say tomorrow down there?" I replied, this time without hesitation, "That the transform is a Fourier, of course." Campbell smiled and chortled, "Good for you! So am I." (p. xvii)

Pribram's (1971) hypothesis was strengthened through a growing appreciation of holography as frequency-superpositioned electromagnetic wave interference (p. 142). Pribram called his approach "the holonomic brain theory," and postulated the importance of the *frequency domain* in future research:

> Essentially, the theory reads that the brain at one stage of processing performs its analyses in the frequency domain . . . a solid body of evidence has accumulated that the auditory, somatosensory, motor, and visual systems of the brain do in fact process, at one or several stages, input from the senses in the frequency domain. (Pribram, 1982, p. 29)

In Pribram's (1990) theory, a pure frequency domain links with the neuronal tissue of the brain through modulating fields of flux within the fine-fibered dendritic webs of the cerebral cortex regions. His paradigm was reinforced at a San Francisco conference during a lecture given by the physicist Geoffrey F. Chew, the head of the UC Berkeley physics department and a former student of Enrico Fermi. Chew presented a conceptual diagram of the Fourier transform process (Figure 3), which perfectly encapsulated what Pribram had by then become familiar with, the Fourier transform (Pribram, 2004a, p. 230). As shown in the figure, the spectral (frequency) domain, located at the left of the diagram, is directly linked to the space-time domain, depicted at the right, bridged by the Fourier transform, operating at the sub-atomic levels predicted by Planck's constant.

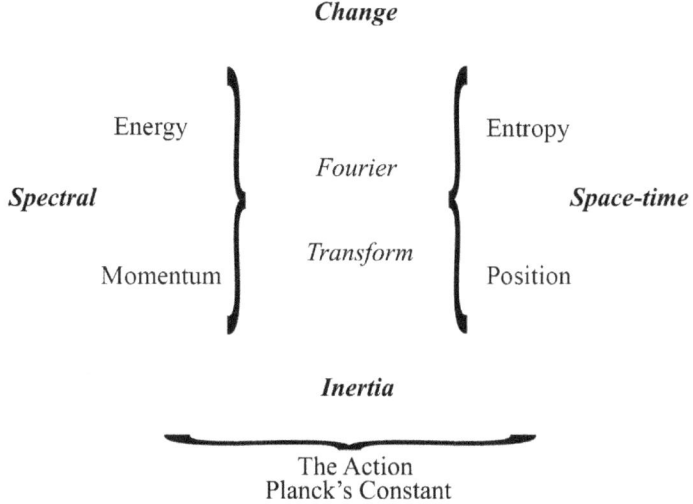

Figure 3. The Dirac Fourier transform diagram. Source: Adapted from Pribram (2004b).

Pribram (2013) asked Chew where he had obtained the diagram, and was told that he had been given the diagram by his colleague at Berkeley, the physicist Henry Stapp, who himself said he had been given it directly from the British theoretical physicist Paul Dirac (1902–1984), one of the original founders of quantum mechanics. Whatever the origin of the figure, Pribram chose to include the diagram in several future papers. In "Consciousness Reassessed," Pribram's (2004b) caption to the figure reads, "The Fourier Transform as the Mediator between Spectral and Spacetime" (p. 8).

In the diagram, the spectral domain is shown at the left and space-time to the right, with the Fourier transform between them. The diagram became foundational to Pribram's understanding. It presents a two–way Fourier transform, operational at the boundary between the two domains, located at an event horizon termed in the diagram, "The Action: Planck's Constant." It is this process of turbulent transformation at the event–horizon that David Bohm and Basil Hiley (1993) termed holomovement or holoflux (p. 382).

The Limits of Space: From the Edge of the Universe to Planck's Constant

The Pribram–Bohm hypothesis holds that the dimensions of space are finite and that space exhibits a limited domain in a quantifiable range. This is consistent with the physics of string theory or M–theory, according to Bernard Carr (2007), Professor of Mathematics and Astronomy at the University of London:

> The Universe may have more than the three dimensions of space that we actually observe, with the extra dimensions being compactified on the Planck scale (the distance of 10^{-35} meters, at which quantum gravity effects become important), so that we do not notice them.... In particular, physics has revealed a unity about the Universe which makes it clear that everything is connected in a way which would have seemed inconceivable a few decades ago. The discovery of dark dimensions through particle physics shakes our view of the nature of reality just as profoundly as the discovery of dark energy through cosmology. (p. 10)

Carr (2007) uses the alchemical image of the ouroboros (Figure 4) to illustrate his GUT theory (Grand Unified Theory) in comparing major scale-dependent structural levels of the physical world: "The significance of the head meeting the tail is that the entire Universe was once compressed to a point of infinite density (or, more strictly, the Planck density)" (p. 13). This archetypal figure implies the interconnectedness of the entire universal process in time and space, presenting a cybernetic feedback loop operational at every scale. Mystics have intuited this ouroboric process symbolized in the images of a snake swallowing its own tail (the image has been found as early as the 14th century BCE in the tomb of Tutankhamun) and it is frequently used to symbolize cybernetic feedback in control and communication theory (Wiener, 1964). While Wiener coined the term *cybernetics*, communication engineers would more commonly see this as metaphor for the "feedback loop," used everywhere in electronic circuit design.

Figure 4. Alchemical Ouroboros (Pelekanos, 1478)

Stretching out this circular cosmic ouroboric serpent from head to tail, one can create an axis of scales that encompasses all of space. In Figure 5 such a scale is drawn starting with the currently estimated diameter of the universe itself at 10^{+25} m, and descending logarithmically down to the Planck length limit at 10^{-35} m. The axis thus spans a total range of 10^{+60} (60 jumps by the power of 10). The Pribram–Bohm hypothesis holds that there, at the very bottom of the linear scale (Figure 5), is to be found the transition bounding the explicate order and the implicate order (Joye, in press, p. 261). Here, at the bottom bound of the spatial scale, space reaches its *end*, according to modern physics; but it also marks the *entry point into* Bohm's "implicate order," what Pribram terms the "frequency domain" (Bohm, 1980; Pribram, 2013).

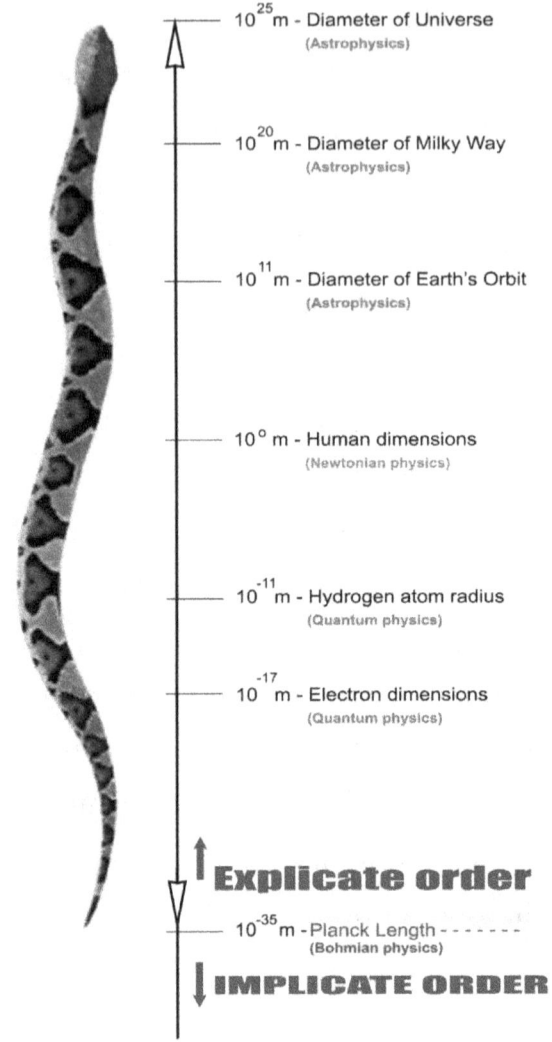

Figure 5. Scales of dimensional space and the explicate/implicate boundary

The implications of this topology are profound. Imagine moving inwardly, from any position in the universe, moving into a spherical bubble, shrinking ever smaller in scale while moving ever closer to the center at the bottom of the spatial scale, following the radial axis inward, ever shrinking downward, and then abruptly reaching the end of the line at the Planck length limit of space, the locus of a spherical shell 10^{-35} meters in diameter, below which space has no meaning. Here a boundary has been reached, an event horizon between space and the implicate order. To understand this, one must realize that the classical Cartesian assumption that space is continuous is *wrong*; there *is* indeed a bottom to space, at least according to physics, below which space no longer has meaning. Here there is a discontinuity, as David Bohm and F. David Peat (1987) explain in describing the granularity of space:

> What of the order between two points in space? The Cartesian order holds that space is continuous. Between any two points, no matter how close they lie, occur an infinite of other points. Between any two neighboring points in this infinity lies another infinity and so on. This notion of continuity is not compatible with the order of quantum theory.... Thus the physicist John Wheeler

has suggested that, at very short distances, continuous space begins to break up into a foam-like structure. Thus the "order between" two points moves from the order of continuity to an order of a discontinuous foam. (pp. 311–312)

Pribram's Spectral Density Flux and the Implicate Order

In 1979, Karl Pribram, at that time a Stanford professor, attended a conference in Cordoba, Spain, where he met David Bohm, a professor of theoretical physics at London University (Cazenave, 1984). During the conference, Pribram (2013) soon realized that David Bohm's model of the implicate order and its projection, or extrusion into space–time, could be seen as entirely compatible with his own holonomic mind/brain theory. Thus began 20 years of correspondence and dialog between David Bohm and Karl Pribram, and the two soon became personal friends.

Pribram (2013) saw in Bohm's theories how the frequency domain flux might be seen to unfold into explicate domain waves of encoded information via the Fourier transform, and he appreciated Bohm's description of how information from the explicate may fold back into the implicate in a bi-directional process. Even more intriguing was Bohm's belief that, "the basic relationship of quantum theory and consciousness is that *they have the implicate order in common* [emphasis added]" (Bohm & Hiley, 1993, pp. 381–382).

Pribram was equally impressed with Bohm's explanation of nonlocality, a major mystery in quantum physics, which Bohm explains as fundamental to the process of folding and unfolding between explicate and implicate orders, allowing for full superpositioned cohesion of frequency information within the implicate order, and even providing a plausible mechanism for Sheldrake's theories of morphogenetic fields and morphic resonance:

> The implicate order can be thought of as a ground beyond time, a totality, out of which each moment is projected into the explicate order. For every moment that is projected out into the explicate there would be another movement in which that moment would be

injected or "introjected" back into the implicate order. If you have a large number of repetitions of this process, you'll start to build up a fairly constant component to this series of projection and injection. That is, a fixed disposition would become established. The point is that, via this process, past forms would tend to be repeated or replicated in the present, and that is very similar to what Sheldrake calls a morphogenetic field and morphic resonance. Moreover, such a field would not be located anywhere. When it projects back into the totality (the implicate order), since no space and time are relevant there, all things of a similar nature might get connected together or resonate in totality. When the explicate order enfolds into the implicate order, which does not have any space, all places and all times are, we might say, merged, so that what happens in one place will interpenetrate what happens in another place. (Bohm & Weber, 1982, pp. 35–36)

Bohm's topology is both supported and extended by Pribram's contention, supported by the diagram handed down from Dirac, that the boundary or event horizon between the two domains, where the action occurs, is at the Planck length, precisely where, as Pribram tells us here, spectral density information translates into space-time ex-formation.

> Matter can be seen as an "ex-formation," an externalized (extruded, palpable, compacted) form of flux. By contrast, thinking and its communication (minding) are the consequence of an internalized (neg-entropic) forming of flux, its "in-formation." My claim is that the basis function from which both matter and mind are "formed" is flux (measured as spectral density). (Pribram, 2004b, p. 13)

This flux or spectral density is for Pribram real, in the same sense that space-time is considered to be real, but this flux is *outside of* or *beyond* space–time. It is in this sense that Pribram made the conceptual leap from considering the Fourier transform as simply a tool of mathematical calculation, to a dawning realization that the reality of the transform implies the ontological *reality* of a domain *outside of space–time*, a transcendent yet ontologically real domain where energy as flux is "measured as spectral density."

Dirac's original diagram can now be extended to include Bohm's two regions of the whole, the implicate order and the explicate order. Figure 6 depicts this expanded diagram.

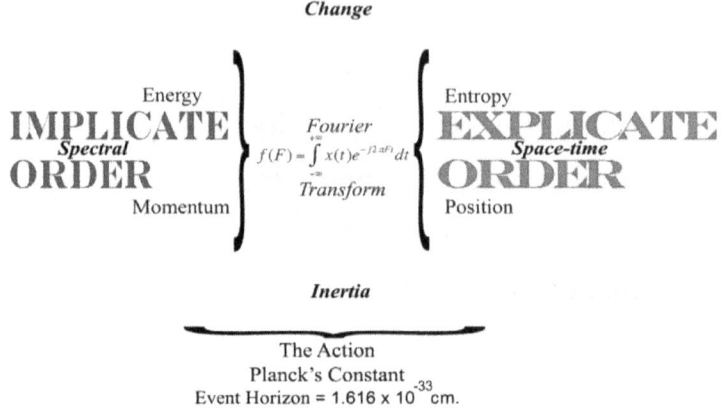

Figure 6. *Dirac's Fourier diagram with David Bohm's topology (Joye, in press)*

An anthropomorphic view of the Pribram's diagram can be seen in Figure 7, where an iris-like lens peering out from the implicate order is maintaining a focus upon and/or projecting a holonomic universe within the explicate order of space–time. This mirrors Karl Pribram's (1991) conceptualization of a lens between the two domains, expressed here in *Brain and Perception*:

These two domains characterize the input to and output from a lens that performs a Fourier transform. On one side of the transform lies the space-time order we ordinarily perceive. On the other side lies a distributed enfolded holographic–like order referred to as the frequency or spectral domain. (p. 70).

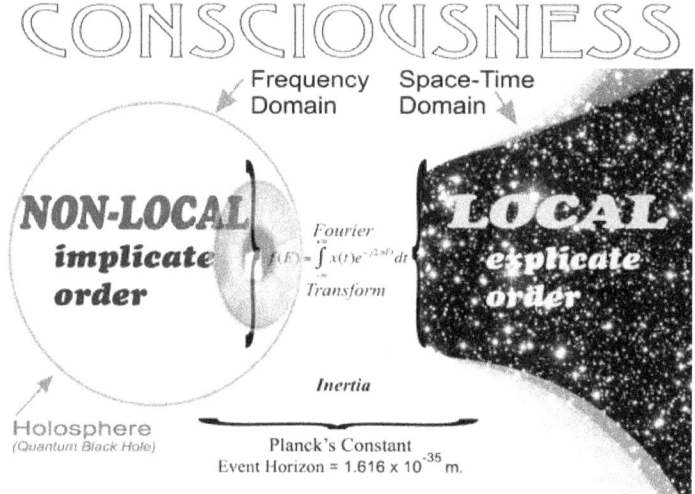

Figure 7. Topology of consciousness

Note that the image of an iris in the diagram appears at the edge of the event horizon of a quantum black hole, or implicate order holosphere. The iris symbolizes consciousness looking *out* from the implicate order *into* space-time via a Fourier transform lensing process. This approach to a topology of consciousness as something that is looking out and seeing itself is supported here by the mathematician G. Spencer-Brown (1972) in *Laws of Form*:

> Now the physicist himself, who describes all this, is, in his own account, constructed of it. He is, in short, made of a conglomeration of the very particulars he describes, no more, no less, bound together by and obeying such general laws as he himself has managed to find and record. Thus we cannot escape the fact that the world we know is constructed in order (and thus in such a way as to be able) to see itself. This is indeed amazing. Not so much in view of what it sees, although this may appear fantastic enough, but in respect of the fact that it can see at all.... But in order to do so, evidently it must first cut itself up into at least one state which sees, and at least one other state which is seen. In this condition it will always partially elude itself. (p. 105)

Cosmology and the Implicate Order

In 1980 Bohm published *Wholeness and the Implicate Order*, and in a section in which he discusses the cosmology of the implicate order, he puts forth a solution to the problem of "zero-point" energy by regarding the Planck length as the shortest wavelength possible:

> If one were to add up the energies of all the "wave-particle" modes of excitation in any region of space, the result would be infinite, because an infinite number of wavelengths is present. However, there is good reason to suppose that one need not keep on adding the energies corresponding to shorter and shorter wavelengths. There may be a certain shortest possible wavelength, so that the total number of modes of excitation, and therefore the energy, would be finite. . . . When this length is estimated it turns out to be about 10^{-35} m. (Bohm, 1980, p. 190)

Bohm (1980) brings up the school of Parmenides and Zeno, which held that all of space is actually a plenum, and he points out that as recently as the last century this same theory was presented in the widely accepted hypothesis of the *ether* (p. 191).

Bohm describes how there is a "holomovement" (p. 151) in this immense sea of "zero-point energy" (p. 190) to be understood as a "undivided flowing movement without borders" (p. 172) and he goes on to state:

> It is being suggested here, then, that what we perceive through the senses as empty space is actually the plenum, which is the ground for the existence of everything, including ourselves. The things that appear to our senses are derivative forms and their true meaning can be seen only when we consider the plenum, in which they are generated and sustained, and into which they must ultimately vanish. (p. 192)

In the Pribram–Bohm cosmology then, the interface or boundary between the space-time explicate domain and the nonlocal, nontemporal implicate domain can be viewed topologically as a holoplenum of holospheres (Figure 8). Here can be found an answer to the "hard problem of consciousness" posed by Chalmers (1995), for it is from *within* each holosphere that consciousness is "peering out" into and "projecting" the space-time explicate, and here Bohm (1980) summarizes his cosmological essay by proposing that "consciousness is to be comprehended in terms of the implicate order, along with reality as a whole" (p. 196) and stating unequivocally that "the implicate order is also its primary and immediate actuality" (p. 197).

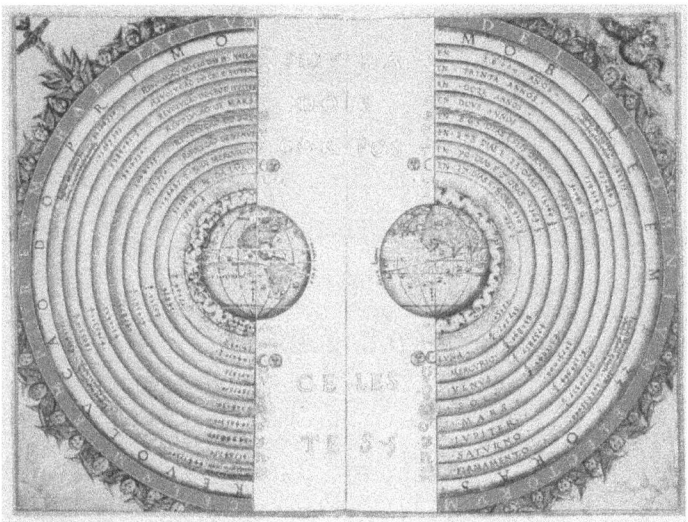

Figure 8. The Ptolemaic Geocentric conception of the Universe. Source: Velho (1568)

In the 3rd century BCE Aristotle (2004) held that the reason an apple falls to the ground is because it seeks its natural place at the center of the universe, and he set forth a geocentric model based upon the following three propositions:

- The Earth is positioned at the center of the universe.
- The Earth is fixed (nonmoving) in relation to the rest of the universe.
- The Earth is special and unique compared to all other heavenly bodies.

Substituting "holosphere" for "Earth" in Aristotle's propositions, each Planck holosphere can be taken as positioned at the center of the universe, each holosphere is fixed (nonmoving) in relation to all other holospheres in the holoplenum, and each holosphere is "special" by virtue of its unique Hilbert space coordinates (Young, 1988).

REFERENCES AND USEFUL BACKGROUND RESOURCES ON CONSCIOUSNESS AND CONTEMPLATION

Aur, Dorian, and Mandar S. Jog. 2010. *Neuroelectrodynamics: Understanding the Brain Language*. Amsterdam: IOS Press.

Baggott, Jim. 2011. *The Quantum Story: A History in 40 Moments*. New York: Oxford University.

Bailes, K. E. 1990. *Science and Russian Culture in an Age of Revolutions: V.I. Vernadsky and His Scientific School, 1863–1945*. Bloomington: Indiana University.

Bailey, Alice A. 1927. *The Light of the Soul: The Yoga Sutras of Patanjali*. New York: Lucis Publishing.

Becker, Robert O. 1990. *Cross Currents: The Perils of Electropollution and the Promise of Electromedicine*. New York: Jeremy Tarcher.

Becker, Robert O., and Gary Selden. 1985. *The Body Electric: Electromagnetism and the Foundation of Life*. New York: Harper.

Bekenstein, Jacob D. 1973. "Black Holes and Entropy." *Physical Review* 7 (8): 2333–46.

Bell, E. T. 1937. *Men of Mathematics*. New York: Simon and Schuster.

Bell, J. S. 1987. *The Speakable and Unspeakable in Quantum Mechanics.* Cambridge: Cambridge University.

Benenson, Walter, John W. Harris, Horst Stocker, and Lutz Holger, eds. 2006. *Handbook of Physics.* New York: Springer Science.

Bergson, Henri. 1911. *Creative Evolution.* Translated by Arthur Mitchell. New York: Henry Holt.

Blinkov, S. M. and I. I. Glezer. 1968. *The Human Brain in Figures and Tables. A Quantitative Handbook.* New York: Plenum.

Block, Ned. 2007. *Consciousness, Function, and Representation: Collected Papers, Vol. 1.* Cambridge: The MIT Press.

Bohm, David. 1951. *Quantum Theory.* New York: Prentiss-Hall.

———. 1952. "A Suggested Interpretation of the Quantum Theory in Terms of 'Hidden Variables,' Vol. 1." *Physical Review* 85 (2): 166–93. Retrieved from http://fma.if.usp.br/~amsilva/Artigos/p166_1.pdf.

———. 1965. *The Special Theory of Relativity.* Philadelphia: John Benjamins.

———. 1978. "The Enfolding-Unfolding Universe: A Conversation with David Bohm." In *The Holographic Paradigm and Other Paradoxes: Exploring the Leading Edge of Science*, edited by Ken Wilber, 44–104. Boulder, CO: Shambhala.

———. 1980. *Wholeness and the Implicate Order*. London: Routledge.

———. 1985. *Unfolding Meaning: A Weekend of Dialogue with David Bohm*. London: Routledge.

———. 1986. "The Implicate Order and the Super-Implicate Order." In *Dialogues with Scientists and Sages: The Search for Unity*, edited by Renée Weber, 23–49. New York: Routledge.

———. 1987a. "Hidden Variables and the Implicate Order." In *Quantum Implications: Essays in Honour of David Bohm,* edited by B. J. Hiley and F. David Peat, 33–45. London: Routledge.

———. 1989. "Meaning and Information." In *The Search for Meaning: The New Spirit in Science and Philosophy*, edited by Paavo Pylkkänen, 43–85. Northamptonshire, England: The Aquarian Press.

———. 1990. *Beyond Limits: A Full Conversation with David Bohm*. Interview by Bill Angelos for Dutch public television. Posted March 5, 2011. Retrieved from http://bohmkrishnamurti.com/beyond-limits/

———. 1990. "A New Theory of the Relationship of Mind and Matter." *Philosophical Psychology* 3 (2): 271–86.

Bohm, David, and Basil J. Hiley. 1993. *The Undivided Universe: An Ontological Interpretation of Quantum Theory*. London: Routledge.

Bohm, David, and J. Krishnamurti. 1985. *The Ending of Time: Where Philosophy and Physics Meet*. New York: Harper Collins.

Bohm, David, and J. Krishnamurti. 1999. *The Limits of Thought: Discussions between J. Krishnamurti and David Bohm*. London: Routledge.

Bohm, David, and F. David Peat. 1987. *Science, Order, and Creativity*. London: Routledge.

Bohm, David, and R. Weber. 1982. "Nature as Creativity." *ReVision* 5 (2): 35–40.

Booth, J. C., S. A. Koren, and Michael A. Persinger. 2005. "Increased Feelings of the Sensed Presence and Increased Geomagnetic Activity at the Time of the Experience During Exposures to Transcerebral Weak Complex Magnetic Fields." *International Journal of Neuroscience* 115 (7): 1039–65.

Born, Irene, trans. 1971. *The Born–Einstein Letters: Friendship, Politics and Physics in Uncertain Times*. New York: Macmillan.

Borsellino, A., and T. Poggio. 1972. "Holographic Aspects of Temporal Memory and Optomotor Responses." *Kybernetik* 10 (1): 58–60.

Brigham, E. O. 2002. *The Fast Fourier Transform*. New York: Prentice-Hall.

Broughton, S. A., and K. Bryan. 2008. *Discrete Fourier Analysis and Wavelets: Applications to Signal and Image Processing*. New York: Wiley.

Browder, Andrew. 1996. *Mathematical Analysis: An Introduction*. New York: Springer-Verlag.

Bruskiewich, Patrick. 2014. *Max Planck and Black-Body Radiation*. Vancouver: Pythagoras Publishing.

Carr1, Bernard J. and Steven B. Giddings. 2005. "Quantum Black Holes." *Scientific American* 292 (5): 30–35.

Cazenave, Michel, ed. 1984. *Science and Consciousness: Two Views of the Universe, Edited Proceedings of the France-Culture and Radio-France Colloquium, Cordoba, Spain*. Oxford: Pergamon.

Chalmers, David J. 1995. "Facing Up to the Problem of Consciousness." *Journal of Consciousness Studies* 2 (3): 200–19.

———. 2010. *The Character of Consciousness*. New York: Oxford University.

Chaudhuri, Haridas. 1954. *The Philosophy of Integralism: The Metaphysical Synthesis in Sri Aurobindo's Teaching*. Pondicherry, India: Sri Aurobindo Ashram Trust.

———. 1960. "The Integral Philosophy of Sri Aurobindo." In *The Integral Philosophy of Sri Aurobindo: A Commemorative Symposium*, edited by Haridas Chaudhuri and Frederic Spiegelberg, 17–34. London: George Allen & Unwin.

———. 1969. *The Integral Philosophy of Sri Aurobindo*. London: George Allen & Unwin.

Chen, Frances F. 2006. *Introduction to Plasma Physics and Controlled Fusion: Vol 1. Plasma Physics*. 2nd ed. New York: Springer.

Cheney, Brainard. 1965. "Has Teilhard de Chardin 'Really' Joined the Within and the Without of Things?" *The Sewanee Review* 73 (2): 217–36.

Cheney, Margaret. 1981. *Tesla: Man Out of Time*. New York: Dorset Press.

Chomsky, Noam. 2000. *New Horizons in the Study of Language and Mind*. Cambridge, England: Cambridge University.

Clark, Walter. 1939. *Photography by Infrared—Its Principles and Applications*. New York: John Wiley & Sons.

Collister, Rupert Clive. 2010. *A Journey in Search of Wholeness and Meaning*. New York: Peter Lang.

Cook, David M. 2002. *The Theory of the Electromagnetic Field*. Englewood Cliffs, NJ: Prentice-Hall.

Corte, Nicolas. 1960. *Pierre Teilhard de Chardin: His Life and Spirit*. New York: Macmillan.

Crease, Robert P. 2008. *The Great Equations: Breakthroughs in Science from Pythagoras to Heisenberg*. New York: W. W. Norton.

Cuénot, Claude. 1965. *Teilhard de Chardin: A Biographical Study*. London: Burnes & Oates.

Darling, David J. 2004. *The Universal Book of Mathematics: From Abracadabra to Zeno's Paradoxes*. Hoboken, NJ: Wiley.

Dawson, Lorne L. 2006. *Comprehending Cults: The Sociology of New Religious Movements*. New York: Oxford University.

Deacon, Terrence W. 2010. "What Is Missing from Theories of Information." In *Information and the Nature of Reality: From Physics to Metaphysics*, edited by Paul Davies and Niels Henrik Gregersen, 123–42. Cambridge, England: Cambridge University.

———. 2012. *Incomplete Nature: How Mind Emerged from Matter*. New York: W. W. Norton.

de Lubac, Henri. 1967. *The Religion of Teilhard de Chardin*. Translated by René Hague. New York: Desclée.

de Terra, Helmut. 1964. *Memories of Teilhard de Chardin*. Translated by J. Maxwell Brownjohn. New York: Harper & Row.

De Valois, Karen K., and Russell L. De Valois. 1988. *Spatial Vision*. New York: Oxford University.

Dennett, Daniel C. 1991. *Consciousness Explained*. New York: Back Bay Books.

Dewey, B. 1985. *The Theory of Laminated Spacetime*. Inverness, CA: Bartholomew.

Dorf, Richard C., ed. 1997. *The Electrical Engineering Handbook*. 2nd ed. Boca Raton, FL: CRC Press.

Drachman, David A. 2005. "Do We Have Brain to Spare?" *Neurology* 64 (6): 2004–5. doi: http://dx.doi.org/10.1212/01.WNL.0000166914.38327.BB.

Dunwell, Frances F. 1980. *The Hudson: America's River*. New York: Columbia University.

Edelman, Gerald M., and Giulio Tononi. 2000. *A Universe of Consciousness: How Matter Becomes Imagination*. New York: Basic Books.

Edmondson, Amy C. 1987. *A Fuller Explanation: The Synergetic Geometry of R. Buckminster Fuller*. Boston: Birkhäuser.

Einstein, Albert. 1979. *Autobiographical Notes*. Peru, IL: Carus.

Eliot, Thomas Stearns. 1943. *Four Quartets*. New York: Harcourt Brace.

———. 1976. *Collected Poems 1909–1962*. New York: Harcourt Brace.

Fechner, Gustav Theodor. 1946. *Religion of a Scientist: Selections from Gustav Theodor Fechner*, New York: Pantheon.

Fellmann, E. A. 2007. *Leonhard Euler*. Translated by E. Gautschi. Basel, Germany: Birkhauser.

Ferrer, Jorge, and Jacob Sherman, eds. 2008. *The Participatory Turn: Spirituality, Mysticism, Religious Studies*. Albany: State University of New York.

Feuerstein, Georg. 1987. *Structures of Consciousness: The Genius of Jean Gebser—An Introduction and Critique*. Lower Lake, CA: Integral.

Feynman, Richard, Robert Leighton, and Matthew Sands. 1964. *The Feynman Lectures on Physics, Vol. 1*. Reading, MA: Addison-Wesley.

Fields, R. Douglas. 2009. *The Other Brain*. New York: Simon & Schuster.

Flanagan, Owen. 1997. "Conscious Inessentialism and the Epiphenomenalist Suspicion." In *The Nature of Consciousness: Philosophical Debates*, edited by Ned Block, Owen Flanagan, and Güven Güzeldere, 357–73. Cambridge, MA: MIT Press.

Fourier, Jean Baptiste Joseph. 1822. *The Analytic Theory of Heat*. Paris: Firmin Didot Père et Fils.

Gabor, Dennis. 1946. "Theory of Communication." *Journal of the Institute of Electrical Engineers* 93: 429–41.

Gao, Shan. 2014. *Dark Energy: From Einstein's Biggest Blunder to the Holographic Universe*. 2nd ed. Seattle, WA: Amazon Kindle Direct.

Garay, Luis J. 1995. "Quantum Gravity and Minimum Length." *International Journal of Modern Physics* 10 (2): 145–65.

Gebser, Jean. 1949. *The Ever-Present Origin: Part One: Foundations of the Aperspectival World*. Translated by J. Keckeis. Stuttgart, Germany: Deutsche Verlags-Anstalt.

———. 1956 (1996). "Cultural Philosophy as Method and Venture." Translated by Georg Feuerstein. *Integrative Explorations: Journal of Culture and Consciousness* 3 (1): 77–82. Retrieved from http://static1.squarespace.com/static/535ef5d8e4b0ab57db4a06c7/t/541f74a0e4b0394ddbf5a040/1411347616917/integrative_explorations_3.pdf.

Geiger, Rudolf, Robert H. Aron, and Paul Todhunter. 2003. *The Climate Near the Ground*. Lanham, MD: Rowman and Littlefield.

Gidley, Jennifer. 2007. "The Evolution of Consciousness as a Planetary Imperative: An Integration of Integral Views." *Integral Review* 3 (5): 4–226. Retrieved from http://integral-review.org/pdf-template-issue.php?pdfName=issue_5_gidley_the_evolution_of_consciousness_as_a_planetary_imperative.pdf.

Globus, Gordon G. 2006. *The Transparent Becoming of World: A Crossing Between Process Philosophy and Quantum Neurophilosophy*. Philadelphia: John Benjamins.

Goswami, Amit. 2000. *The Visionary Window: A Quantum Physicist's Guide to Enlightenment*. Wheaton, IL: Quest Books.

Gott, J. Richard III, Mario Jurić, David Schlegel, and Fiona Hoyle. 2005. "A Map of the Universe." *The Astrophysics Journal* 624 (2): 463–514.

Haisch, Bernard. 2010. *The Purpose-Guided Universe: Believing in Einstein, Darwin, and God*. Pompton Plains, NJ: New Page Books.

Hameroff, Stuart R. 2015. "Is Your Brain Really a Computer, or Is It a Quantum Orchestra?" *Huffington Post*, July 9. Retrieved from http://www.huffingtonpost.com/stuart-hameroff/is-your-brain-really-a-co_b_7756700.html.

Hameroff, Stuart, and Roger Penrose. 1996. "Conscious Events as Orchestrated Space-Time Selections." *Journal of Consciousness Studies* 3 (1): 35–53.

Hameroff, Stuart R., Travis J. A. Craddock, and Jack A. Tuszynski. 2014. "Quantum Effects in the Understanding of Consciousness." *Journal of Integrative Neuroscience* (13) 2: 229–52. doi:10.1142/S0219635214400093.

Harnad, Stevan. 1994. "Why and How We Are Not Zombies." *Journal of Consciousness Studies* 1 (1): 18–23.

Havelka, D., M. Cifra, O. Kucera, J. Pokorny, and J. Vrba. 2011. "High-frequency Electric Field and Radiation Characteristics of Cellular Microtubule Network." *Journal of Theoretical Biology* 286 (7): 31–40.

Heehs, Peter. 2008. *The Lives of Sri Aurobindo*. New York: Columbia University.

Herculano-Houzel, Suzana. 2009. "The Human Brain in Numbers: A Linearly Scaled-up Primate Brain." Frontiers in Human Neuroscience (3) 31: 1–11. doi: 10.3389/neuro.09.031.2009

Hertz, Heinrich. 1893. *Electric Waves: Being Researches On the Propagation of Electric Action with Finite Velocity Through Space*. London: MacMillan.

Hiley, B. J., and F. David Peat, eds. 1987. *Quantum Implications: Essays in Honour of David Bohm*. London: Routledge.

Hiley, B. J., and F. David Peat, eds. 1987. "The Development of David Bohm's Ideas from the Plasma to the Implicate Order." In *Quantum Implications: Essays Honour of David Bohm*, edited by B. J. Hiley and F. David Peat, 1–32. London: Routledge.

Horne, Alistair. 1962. *The Price of Glory: Verdun 1916*. New York: St. Martin's Press.

Howell, Kenneth B. 2001. *Principles of Fourier Analysis*. Boca Raton, FL: Chapman & Hall.

Ishikawa, Hiroaki, and Wallace F. Marshall. "Ciliogenesis: Building the Cell's Antenna." *Nature Reviews Molecular Biology* 12 (4): 222-34. dos:10.1038/nrm3085

Jibu, Mari, and Kunio Yasue. 1995. *Quantum Brain Dynamics and Consciousness*. Philadelphia: John Benjamins.

———. 2003. "Quantum Brain Dynamics and Quantum Field Theory." In *Brain and Being: At the Boundary Between Science, Philosophy, Language and Arts*, edited by Gordon Globus, Karl Pribram, and Giuseppe Vitiello, 267–90. Philadelphia: John Benjamins.

Johnston, Sean F. 2006. *Holographic Visions: A History of New Science*. New York: Oxford University.

Jung, C. G. 1968. *Psychology and Alchemy*. Vol. 12 of *The Collected Works of C. G. Jung*. Edited and translated by Gerald Adler and R. F. C. Hull. 2nd ed. Princeton, NJ: Princeton University.

———. (1946) 1969. "On the Nature of the Psyche." In Vol. 8 of *The Collected Works of C. G. Jung*, translated by R. F. C. Hull, 159–234. 2nd ed. Princeton, NJ: Princeton University.

Kachris, Christoforos, Keren Bergman, and Ioannis Tomkos. 2012. *Optical Interconnects for Future Data Center Networks*. New York. Springer.

Kafatos, Menas, Rudolph E. Tanzi, and Deepak Chopra. 2011. "How Consciousness Becomes the Physical Universe." *Journal of Cosmology* (14): 1318–1328. Retrieved from http://journalofcosmology.com/Consciousness140.html.

King, Ursula. 1996. *Spirit of Fire: The Life and Vision of Teilhard de Chardin*. New York: Orbis Books.

———. 1999. *Pierre Teilhard de Chardin: Writings Selected with an Introduction by Ursula King*. New York: Orbis Books.

Köhler, Wolfgang. 1940. *Dynamics in Psychology: Vital Applications of Gestalt Psychology*. New York: W. W. Norton.

———. 1969. *The Task of Gestalt Psychology*. New Jersey: Princeton University.

Köhler, Wolfgang, and Mary Henle. 1971. *The Selected Papers of Wolfgang Köhler*. New York: W. W. Norton.

Kropf, Richard W. 2014. "Searching for Soul: Teilhard, De Lubac, Rahner, and the Evolutionary Quest for Immortality." *Teilhard Studies* 69 (4): 1–28.

Kuehn, Kerry. 2014. *A Student's Guide Through the Great Physics Texts, Vol. 1: The Heavens and The Earth*. New York: Springer.

Kuo, Franklin. 1962. *Network Analysis and Synthesis*. New York: John Wiley & Sons.

Lashley, Karl. 1951. "An Examination of the Electric Field Theory of Cerebral Integration." *Psychological Review* 58: 123–36.

———. 1950. "In Search of the Engram." *Symposium of the Society for Experimental Biology* 4: 454–82.

László, Ervin. 2006. *Science and the Re-Enchantment of the Cosmos: The Rise of the Integral Vision of Reality*. Rochester, VT: Inner Traditions.

———. 2007. *Science and the Akashic Field: An Integral Theory of Everything*. Rochester, VT: Inner Traditions.

———. 2014a. *The Immortal Mind: Science and the Continuity of Consciousness beyond the Brain*. Rochester, VT: Inner Traditions.

———. 2014b. *The Self-Actualizing Cosmos: The Akasha Revolution in Science and Human Consciousness*. Rochester, VT: Inner Traditions.

Leckie, Robert. 1987. *Delivered from Evil: The Saga of World War II*. New York: Harper & Row.

Leith, Emmet N., and J. Upatnieks. 1962. "Reconstructed Wavefronts and Communication Theory." *Journal of the Optical Society of America* 52 (10): 1123–30.

———. 1965. "Photography by Laser." *Scientific American* 212 (6): 24–35.

Leroy, Pierre. 1960. "Teilhard de Chardin: The Man." Introduction to *The Divine Milieu,* by Teilhard de Chardin, 13–42. New York: Harper & Row.

Lilly, John. 1967. *The Mind of the Dolphin: A Nonhuman Intelligence.* New York: Doubleday.

———. 1977. *The Deep Self: Consciousness Exploration in the Isolation Tank.* New York: Simon & Schuster.

Livio, Mario. 2003. *The Golden Ratio: The Story of Phi, the World's Most Astonishing Number.* New York: Broadway Books.

Lundqvist, Stig, ed. 1992. *Nobel Lectures, Physics 1971–1980.* Singapore: World Scientific.

MacKenna, Stephen. 1992. *Plotinus: The Enneads.* New York: Larson Publications.

Malinski, Tadeusz. 1960. *Chemistry of the Heart.* Ohio: Biochemistry Research Laboratory. Retrieved from http://hypertextbook.com/facts/2003/IradaMuslumova.shtml

McCraty, Rollin. 2003. *The Energetic Heart: Bioelectromagnetic Interactions Within and Between People*. Boulder Creek, CA: Institute of HeartMath.

McCraty, Rollin, M. Atkinson, D. Tomasino, and R. T. Bradley. 2009. "The Coherent Heart: Heart–Brain Interactions, Psychophysiological Coherence, and the Emergence of System-Wide Order." *Integral Review* 5 (9): 10–115.

McCraty, Rollin, Annette Deyhle, and Doc Childre. 2012. "The Global Coherence Initiative: Creating a Coherent Planetary Standing Wave." *Global Advances in Health and Medicine* 1 (1): 64–77. Retrieved from https://www.heartmath.org/assets/uploads/2015/01/gci-creating-a-coherent-planetary-standing-wave.pdf.

McFadden, Johnjoe. 2002a. "The Conscious Electromagnetic Information (CEMI) Field Theory: The Hard Problem Made Easy." *Journal of Consciousness Studies* 9 (8): 45–60.

———. 2002b. "Synchronous Firing and Its Influence on the Brain's Electromagnetic Field: Evidence for an Electromagnetic Field Theory of Consciousness." *Journal of Consciousness Studies* 9 (4): 23–50.

———. 2006. "The CEMI Field Theory." In *The Emerging Physics of Consciousness*, edited by Jack A. Tuszynski, 385–404. Berlin: Springer-Verlag.

———. 2007. "Conscious Electromagnetic Field Theory." *NeuroQuantology* 5 (3): 262–70.

McGinn, Colin. 1997. "Consciousness and Space." In *Explaining Consciousness: The Hard Problem*, edited by Jonathan Shear, 97–108. Boston: MIT.

McIntosh, Steve. 2007. *Integral Consciousness and the Future of Evolution*. St. Paul, MN: Paragon House.

Merrell-Wolff, Franklin. 1973. *The Philosophy of Consciousness Without an Object: Reflections on the Nature of Transcendental Consciousness*. New York: Julian Press.

Milonni, Peter W., and Joseph E. Eberly. 2010. *Laser Physics*. Hoboken, NJ: John Wiley & Sons.

Morgan, Conway Lloyd. 1978. *Emergent Evolution: Gifford Lectures, 1921–22*. New York: Simon & Schuster.

Morin, Edgar. 1999. *Seven Complex Lessons in Education for the Future*. Translated by Nidra Poller. Paris: UNESCO.

Netter, F. H. 1972. *A Compilation of Paintings of the Normal and Pathologic Anatomy of the Nervous System*. Summit, NJ: CIBA.

Neville, Katherine. 1992. "Saral and David Bohm, Prague, June 1992" (photograph). Retrieved from http://www.karlpribram.com/photos/.

Nilson, Arthur R., and J. L. Hornung. 1943. *Practical Radio Communication: Principles, Systems, Equipment, Operation, Including Very High and Ultra High Frequencies and Frequency Modulation*. 2nd ed. New York: McGraw-Hill.

Nishikawa, K., and M. Wakatani. 2000. *Plasma Physics*. Berlin: Springer-Verlag.

Nunez, Paul L. 2010. *Brain, Mind, and the Structure of Reality*. New York: Oxford University.

Oates, B. 1971. *Celebrating the Dawn: Maharishi Mahesh Yogi and the TM Technique*. New York: Putnam Books.

Ouspensky, P. D. 1949. *In Search of the Miraculous: Fragments of an Unknown Teaching*. London: Harcourt.

Oyster, Clyde W. 1999. *The Human Eye: Structure and Function*. Sunderland, MA: Sinauer Associates.

Peat, F. David. 1997. *Infinite Potential: The Life and Times of David Bohm*. Reading, MA: Addison-Wesley.

Penfield, Wilder. 1975. *The Mystery of the Mind: A Critical Study of Consciousness and the Human Brain*. Princeton, NH: Princeton University.

Penrose, Sir Roger. 1989. *The Emperor's New Mind: Concerning Computers, Minds and the Laws of Physics*. New York: Oxford University.

Penrose, R., Stuart Hameroff, and S. Kak, eds. 2011. *Consciousness and the Universe: Quantum Physics, Evolution, Brain & Mind* (Contents selected from Volumes 3 and 14, *Journal of Cosmology*). Cambridge: Cosmology Science.

Persinger, Michael A. 2014. "Schumann Resonance Frequencies Found Within Quantitative Electroencephalographic Activity: Implications for Earth-Brain Interactions." *International Letters of Chemistry, Physics and Astronomy* 30: 24–32. doi:10.18052/www.scipress.com/ILCPA.30.24.

Pizzi, Rita, Giuliano Strini, Silvia Fiorentini, Valeria Pappalardo, and Massimo Pregnolato. 2010. "Evidences of New Biophysical Properties of Microtubules." In *Artificial Neural Networks*, edited by Seoyun J. Kwon. New York: Nova Science Publishers, 1–17. Retrieved from https://air.unimi.it/retrieve/handle/2434/167480/168890/evidences.pdf.

Planck, Max. 1901. "On the Law of Distribution of Energy in the Normal Spectrum." *Annalen der Physik.* 309 (3): 553–63.

Pockett, Susan. 2000. *The Nature of Consciousness: A Hypothesis*. Lincoln, NE: Writers Club.

Pribram, Karl H. 1962. "The Neuropsychology of Sigmund Freud." In *Experimental Foundations of Clinical Psychology*, edited by Arthur J. Bachrach, 442–68. New York: Basic Books.

———. 1971. *Languages of the Brain: Experimental Paradoxes and Principles in Neuropsychology*. Englewood Cliffs, NJ: Prentice-Hall.

———. 1982. "What the Fuss is All About." In *The Holographic Paradigm and Other Paradoxes*, edited by Ken Wilber, 27–34. Boulder: Shambhala.

———. 1984. "Mind, Brain and Consciousness: The Organization of Competence and Conduct." In *Science and Consciousness: Two Views of the Universe*, edited by Julian Davidson and Richard Davidson, 115–32. New York: Springer.

———. 1990. "Prolegomenon for a Holonomic Brain Theory." In *Synergetics of Cognition*, edited by H. Haken, 150–84. Berlin: Springer-Verlag.

———. 1991. *Brain and Perception: Holonomy and Structure in Figural Processing*. Hillsdale, NJ: Lawrence Erlbaum.

———. 2004a. "Brain and Mathematics." In *Brain and Being: At the Boundary Between Science, Philosophy, Language and Arts*, edited by Gordon Globus, Karl Pribram, and Giuseppe Vitiello, 215–40. Philadelphia: John Benjamins.

———. 2004b. "Consciousness Reassessed." *Mind and Matter* 2 (1): 7–35.

———. 2011. "Karl Pribram: Bibliography." Retrieved from http://www.karlpribram.com/bibliography/.

———. 2013. *The Form Within: My Point of View*. Westport, CT: Prospecta Press.

Pribram, Karl H., A. Sharafat, and G. Beekman. 1984. "Frequency Encoding in Motor Systems." In *Human Motor Actions: Bernstein Reassessed*, edited by H. T. A. Whiting, 121–56. Amsterdam: Elsevier Science Publishers.

Prigogine, Ilya. 2015. *Modern Thermodynamics: From Heat Engines to Dissipative Structures*. Hoboken, NJ: John Wiley & Sons.

Pylkkänen, Paavo. 2007. *Mind, Matter, and the Implicate Order*. New York: Springer.

Radhakrishnan, Sarvepalli, ed. 1952. *History of Philosophy Eastern and Western, Vol. 2*. London: George Allen & Unwin.

Ramon y Cajal, Santiago. 2007. "File: Purkinje_cell_by_Cajal.png" (graphic file). January 30, 2016. Wikimedia Commons. Retrieved from https://commons.wikimedia.org/wiki/File:Purkinje_cell_by_Cajal.png.

Raven, Charles E. 1962. *Teilhard de Chardin: Scientist and Seer*. London: William Collins Sons.

Rescher, Nicholas, ed. 1991. *G. W. Leibniz's Monadology: An Edition for Students*. Pittsburgh: University of Pittsburgh.

Ringbauer, M., B. Duffus, C. Branciard, E. G. Cavalcanti, A. G. White, and A. Fedrizzi. 2015. "Measurements On the Reality of the Wavefunction." *Nature Physics* 11 (2): 249–254. doi:10.1038/nphys3233.

Romanes, G. J., ed. 1964. *Cunningham's Textbook of Anatomy*. 10th ed. New York: Oxford University.

Rose, D. 2006. *Consciousness: Philosophical, Psychological and Neural Theories*. New York: Oxford University.

Ruhenstroth-Bauer, Gerhard. 1993. "Influence of the Earth's Magnetic Field on Resting and Activated EEG Mapping in Normal Subjects." *International Journal of Neuroscience* 73 (3): 331–49.

Runehov, Anne, and Luis Oviedo, eds. 2013. *Encyclopedia of Sciences and Religions*. Dordrecht, Netherlands: Springer Netherlands.

Ruppert, L. 1956. *History of the International Electrotechnical Commission*. Geneva: Central Bureau of the IEC.

Samson, Paul R., and David Pitt, eds. 1999. *The Biosphere and Noosphere Reader: Global Environment, Society and Change*. New York: Routledge.

Sentman, Davis D. 1995. "Schumann Resonances." In *Handbook of Atmospheric Electrodynamics, Vol. 1*, edited by Hans Volland, 267–96. Boca Raton, FL: CRC Press.

Shannon, C. E. 1948. "A Mathematical Theory of Communication." *Bell System Technical Journal* 27: 623–56.

Sheldrake, Rupert. 1981. *A New Science of Life: The Hypothesis of Morphic Resonance*. Rochester, VT: Park Street.

———. 1988. *The Presence of the Past: Morphic Resonance and the Habits of Nature*. New York: Times Books.

———. 1989. *Morphic Resonance: The Nature of Formative Causation*. Rochester, VT: Park Street.

Skrbina, David. 2007. *Panpsychism in the West*. Cambridge, MA: MIT Press.

Smolin, Lee. 2013. *Time Reborn*. London: Penguin Books.

Speaight, Robert. 1967. *The Life of Teilhard de Chardin*. New York: Harper & Row.

Sperry, Roger W., N. Miner, and R.E. Myers. 1955. "Visual Pattern Perception Following Subpial Slicing and Tantalum Wire Implantations in the Visual Cortex." *Journal of Comparative and Physiological Psychology* 48 (1): 50–58.

Squire, Larry R., ed. 1998. *The History of Neuroscience in Autobiography, Vol. 2*. London: Academic Press.

Stanford Daily. 1977. "Scientists to Speak." 172 (2): 8.

Stapp, Henry P. 2009. *Mind, Matter, and Quantum Mechanics*. 3rd ed. New York: Springer-Verlag.

Steiner, Rudolf. 1959. *Cosmic Memory: Prehistory of Earth and Man*, translated by K. E. Zimmer. San Francisco: Harper & Row.

Stuart, C.I.J., Y. Takahashi, and H. Umezawa .1979. "Mixed System Brain Dynamics: Neural Memory as a Macroscopic Ordered State." *Foundations of Physics* (9): 301–7.

Susskind, Leonard. 2008. *The Black Hole War: My Battle with Stephen Hawking to Make the World Safe for Quantum Mechanics*. New York: Little, Brown and Company.

Taimni, I. K. 1969. *Man, God and the Universe*. Madras, India: The Theosophical Society.

Talbot, Michael. 1992. *The Holographic Universe*. New York: Harper Collins.

Teilhard de Chardin, Pierre. (1916) 1968. "Cosmic Life." In *Writings in Time of War*, translated by René Hague, 14–71. London: William Collins Sons.

———. (1916) 1978. "Christ in Matter." In *The Heart of Matter*, translated by René Hague, 61–67. New York: Harcourt Brace Jovanovich.

———. (1917) 1978. "Nostalgia for the Front." In *The Heart of Matter*, translated by René Hague, 168–81. New York: Harcourt Brace Jovanovich.

———. (1918a) 1978. "The Great Monad." In *The Heart of Matter*, translated by René Hague, 182–95. New York: Harcourt Brace Jovanovich.

———. (1918b) 1978. "My Universe." In *The Heart of Matter*, translated by René Hague, 196–208. New York: Harcourt Brace Jovanovich. ———. (1923) 1966. "Hominization." In *The Vision of the Past*, translated by J. M. Cohen, 51–79. New York: Harper & Row.

———. (1931) 1969. "The Spirit of the Earth." In *Human Energy*, translated by J. M. Cohen, 93–112. New York: Harcourt Brace Jovanovitch.

———. (1937) 1969. "The Phenomenon of Spirituality." In *Human Energy*, translated by J. M. Cohen, 93–112. New York: Harcourt Brace Jovanovitch.

———. (1941) 1976. "The Atomism of Spirit." In *Activation of Energy*, translated by René Hague, 21–57. London: William Collins Sons.

———. (1942) 1976. "Man's Place in the Universe." In *The Vision of the Past*, translated by J.M. Cohen, 216–33. New York: Harper & Row.

———. (1943) 1969. "Human Energy." In *Human Energy*, translated by J. M. Cohen, 113–62. New York: Harcourt Brace Jovanovitch.

———. (1944) 1976. "Centrology: An Essay in a Dialectic of Union." In *Activation of Energy*, translated by René Hague, 97–127. London: William Collins Sons.

———. (1945) 1959. "Life and the Planets." In *The Future of Man*, translated by Norman Denny, 97–123. New York: Harper & Row.

———. (1946) 1976. "Outline of a Dialectic of Spirit." In *Activation of Energy*, translated by René Hague, 143–51. London: William Collins Sons.

———. (1948) 1975. "My Fundamental Vision." In *Toward the Future*, translated by René Hague, 163–208. London: William Collins Sons.

———. (1949) 1956. "The Formation of the Noosphere II." In *Man's Place in Nature: The Human Zoological Group*, translated by René Hague, 96–121. New York: Harper & Row.

———. (1950a) 1978. "The Heart of Matter." In *The Heart of Matter*, translated by René Hague, 15–79. New York: Harcourt Brace Jovanovich.

———. (1950b) 1976. "The Zest for Living." In *Activation of Energy*, translated by René Hague, 229–43. London: William Collins Sons.

———. (1951a) 1976. "The Convergence of the Universe." In *Activation of Energy*, translated by René Hague, 281–96. London: William Collins Sons.

———. (1951b) 1976. "A Mental Threshold Across Our Path: From Cosmos to Cosmogenesis." In *Activation of Energy*, translated by René Hague, 251–68. London: William Collins Sons.

———. (1951c) 1975. "Some Notes on the Mystical Sense: An Attempt at Clarification" In *Toward the Future*, translated by René Hague, 209–11. London: William Collins Sons.

———. (1953a) 1976. "The Activation of Human Energy." In *Activation of Energy*, translated by René Hague, 359–93. London: William Collins Sons.

———. (1953b) 1976. "The Energy of Evolution." In *Activation of Energy*, translated by René Hague, 359–72. London: William Collins Sons.

———. (1953c) 1976. "The Stuff of the Universe." In *Activation of Energy*, translated by René Hague, 375–83. London: William Collins Sons.

———. (1953d) 1976. "Universalization and Union." In *Activation of Energy*, translated by René Hague, 77–95. London: William Collins Sons.

———. (1954) 1956. "The Nature of the Point Omega." In *The Appearance of Man*, translated by J.M. Cohen, 271–73. New York: Harper & Row.

———. (1955) 1976. "The Death-Barrier and Co-Reflection, or the Imminent Awakening of Human Consciousness to the Sense of Its Irreversibility." In *Activation of Energy*, translated by René Hague, 395–406. London: William Collins Sons.

———. 1956. *The Appearance of Man*. Translated by J. M. Cohen. New York: Harper & Row.

———. 1959. *The Phenomenon of Man*. Translated by Bernard Wall. New York: Harper & Row.

———. 1960. *The Divine Milieu*. New York: Harper & Row.

———. 1961. *The Making of a Mind: Letters from a Soldier–Priest 1914–1919*. Translated by Rene Hague. New York: Harper & Row.

———. 1962. *Letters from a Traveler*. New York: Harper & Row.

———. 1965. *Building the Earth*. Translated by Noël Lindsay. Wilkes-Barre, PA: Dimension Books.

———. 1968. *Letters to Two Friends 1926–1952*. New York: New American Library.

———. 1969a. *Human Energy*. Translated by J. M. Cohen. New York: Harcourt Brace Jovanovitch.

———. 1969b. *Letters to Leontine Zanta*. Translated by Bernard Wall. New York: Harper & Row.

———. 1971a. *Christianity and Evolution: Reflections on Science and Religion*. Translated by René Hague. London: William Collins Sons.

———. 1971b. *Pierre Teilhard de Chardin: L'Oeuvre Scientifique*. Edited by Nicole and Karl Schmitz-Moormann. 10 vols. Munich: Walter-Verlag.

———. 1972. *Lettres Intimes de Teilhard de Chardin a Auguste Valensin, Bruno de Solages, et Henri de Lubac 1919–1955*. Paris: Aubier Montaigne.

———. 1976. *Activation of Energy*. Translated by Rene Hague. London: William Collins Sons.

———. 1978. *The Heart of Matter*. Translated by René Hague. New York: Harcourt Brace Jovanovich.

———. 2003. *The Human Phenomenon*. Translated and edited by Sarah Appleton-Weber. Portland, OR: Sussex Academic. First published 1955.

Tjlaxs. 2005. "File:YoungJamesClerkMaxwell.jpg" (graphic file). November 28, 2015. Wikimedia Commons. https://commons.wikimedia.org/wiki/File:YoungJamesClerkMaxwell.jpg.

Todeschi, Kevin J. 1998. *Edgar Cayce on the Akashic Records: The Book of Life*. Virginia Beach, VA: A. R. E. Press.

Turgeon, Mary Louise. 2004. *Clinical Hematology: Theory and Procedures*. Baltimore, MD: Lippincott Williams & Wilkins.

Tudzynski, P., T. Correia, and U. Keller. 2001. "Biotechnology and Genetics of Ergot Alkaloids." *Applied Microbiology and Biotechnology*, 57: 593–605. doi:10.1007/s002530100801.

Tuszyński, Jack A., ed. 2006. *The Emerging Physics of Consciousness*. New York: Springer-Verlag.

Van Dokkum, Pieter G., and Charlie Conroy. 2010. "A Substantial Population of Low-Mass Stars in Luminous Elliptical Galaxies." *Nature* 468 (7326): 940–42. doi:10.1038/nature09578.

Vejvoda, Stanislav. 2003. *17th International Conference on Structural Mechanics in Reactor Technology*. Prague, Czech Republic: Czech Standard Institute.

Vernadsky, Vladimir Ivanovich. 1998. *The Biosphere*. Translated by D. B. Langmuir. New York: Springer-Verlag.

Walker, J. Samuel. 2004. *Three Mile Island: A Nuclear Crisis in Historical Perspective*. Berkeley: University of California Press.

Warren, Stephen G., and Richard E. Brandt. 2008. "Optical Constants of Ice from the Ultraviolet to the Microwave: A Revised Compilation." *Journal of Geophysical Research*, 113 (D14): 1047–57.

Wasson, Tyler, and Gert Brieger. 1987. *Nobel Prize Winners: A Biographical Dictionary*. New York: H. W. Wilson.

Weber, Renée. 1982. "The Physicist and the Mystic—Is a Dialogue Between Them Possible?" In *The Holographic Paradigm and Other Paradoxes: Exploring the Leading Edge of Science*, edited by Ken Wilber, 187–214. Boulder, CO: Shambhala.

Weisenberger, Drew. n.d. "Jefferson Lab Questions and Answers: How Many Atoms Are There in the World?" Retrieved January 20, 2016 from http://education.jlab.org/qa/mathatom_05.html

Wheeler, John Archibald. 1990. *Information, Physics, Quantum: The Search for Links*. Austin, TX: University of Texas.

———. 1990. *A Journey into Gravity and Spacetime*. New York: Scientific American.

———. 1998. *Geons, Black Holes, and Quantum Foam: A Life in Physics*. New York: W. W. Norton.

Whicher, Ian. 1997. "Nirodha, Yoga Praxis, and the Transformation of the Mind." *Journal of Indian Philosophy* 25 (1): 1–67.

Whitehead, Alfred North. 1978. *Process and Reality: An Essay in Cosmology. Gifford Lectures*, 1927–28. New York: Simon & Schuster.

Wick, Manfred, Wulf Pinggera, and Paul Lehmann. 2003. *Clinical Aspects and Laboratory Iron Metabolism*. Vienna, Austria: Springer-Verlag.

Wiener, Norbert. 1948. *Cybernetics or Control and Communication in the Animal and the Machine*. Cambridge, MA: MIT Press.

Wilber, Ken, ed. 1982. *The Holographic Paradigm and Other Paradoxes: Exploring the Leading Edge of Science*. Boulder, CO: Shambhala.

———, ed. 1985. *Quantum Questions: Mystical Writings of the World's Great Physicists*. Boston: Shambhala.

———. 1996. *A Brief History of Everything*. Boston: Shambhala.

———. 1997. *Integral Spirituality: A Startling New Role for Religion in the Modern and Postmodern World*. Boston: Integral Books.

Wiltschko, Wolfgang, and Roswitha Wiltschko. 2008. "Magnetic Orientation and Magnetoreception in Birds and Other Animals." *Journal of Comparative Physiology A: Neuroethology, Sensory, Neural, and Behavioral Physiology* 191 (8): 675–93. doi:10.1007/s00359-005-0627-7.

Wong, Eva. 1997. *The Shambhala Guide to Taoism*. Boston: Shambhala.

Woolf, N. J. 2006. "Microtubules in the Cerebral Cortex: Role in Memory and Consciousness." In *The Emerging Physics of Consciousness*, edited by Jack A. Tuszyński, 49–94. New York: Springer-Verlag.

Yau, Shing-Tung, and Steve Nadis. 2010. *The Shape of Inner Space: String Theory and the Geometry of the Universe's Hidden Dimensions*. New York: Basic Books.

Zimmer C. 2009. "Origins: On The Origin of Eukaryotes." *Science* 325 (5941): 666–68.

Zizzi, Paola. 2006. "Consciousness and Logic in a Quantum Computing Universe." In *The Emerging Physics of Consciousness*, edited by Jack A. Tuszyński, 457–81. New York: Springer-Verlag.

References

[1] This higher Being has been called different things in different cultures, ages, and religions: "God the Father," "Allah," "Ayn Sof," "Yahweh," "Brahma," "Buddha," "Avalokiteshvara," "Elohim," "Heavenly Father," or in the Jungian sense, the larger Self.

[2] The *Patrologia Latina*, widely used by scholars of the Middle Ages, is an enormous collection of Latin writings that contains 46 works by Hugh of Saint Victor, and this is not his full collection.

[3] This is practice called *lectio divina*, primarily a technique used by monks and priests.

[4] Techniques of meditation are intermediate practices leading up to the breakthrough into contemplative stages, and include a wide range of physical, psychophysical, or purely cognitive practices (e.g., "mindfulness," "prayer," "mantra," "liturgy," "TM," "hatha yoga," "tai chi chuan," etc.)

[5] I was eighteen when I first learned of the famous American psychologist William James (1842-1910) and his practice of "introspection," his approach to exploring and studying consciousness "first-hand."

[6] The use of *Tantric* here (as in "Tantric techniques"), discussed at length earlier in the book, should be understood as "practical, effective, achievable, psychophysical, neuroanatomical, repeatable" techniques.

⁷ *Temenos* (Greek): a sacred space, a sanctuary; C.G. Jung relates a *temenos* to a "magic circle" in which an encounter with the unconscious can be had and where these unconscious contents can safely be brought into the light of consciousness.

⁸ *Neuroplasticity*, also known as neural plasticity, or brain plasticity, is the ability of neural networks in the brain to change through growth and reorganization. These changes range from individual neurons making new connections, to systematic adjustments like cortical remapping.

⁹ Like several software apps, "Insight Timer" automatically saves one's meditation time, charts progress over time, and allows the user to create or join groups which can "see each other" during meditation periods and share statistics (i.e., how many minutes, how often, who was meditating at the same time I was meditating, etc.). It also allows one to set a wide range of audio bell sounds during a meditation period as used by Buddhist monks in Tibet and India.

¹⁰ John Main (1926-1982) was a Roman Catholic priest and monk who, during an early assignment to Kuala Lumpur prior to ordination as a priest, was taught the use of a *mantra* to reach meditative stillness. In 1972 Main returned to England where he began teaching the practice of using a Christian *mantra* at his monastery in West London.

¹¹ See my book *Exploring the Noosphere: Teilhard de Chardin*.

www.ingramcontent.com/pod-product-compliance
Lightning Source LLC
Chambersburg PA
CBHW070449050426
42451CB00015B/3413